EXPLORING the Sunday Gospel

A Lectionary-Based Guide for Groups (Cycle C)

Rev. Joseph T. Sullivan

LIGUORI
PUBLICATIONS

ONE LIGUORI DRIVE
LIGUORI PUBLICATIONS
LIGUORI, MO 63057-9999
(314) 464-2500

Imprimi Potest:
James Shea, C.SS.R.
Provincial, St. Louis Province
The Redemptorists

Imprimatur:
Monsignor Maurice F. Byrne
Vice Chancellor, Archdiocese of St. Louis
ISBN 0-89243-520-8
Library of Congress Catalog Card Number: 92-75940

Cover and interior design by Christine Kraus

Contents

INTRODUCTION

The Spirit that refreshed the Church through the Second Vatican Council calls us to a respectful awareness of Scripture and an application of the gospel in our daily lives:

"Seeing that, in sacred Scripture, God speaks through men in human fashion, it follows that the interpreter of sacred Scriptures, if he is to ascertain what God has wished to communicate to us, should carefully search out the meaning which the sacred writers really had in mind, that meaning which God had thought well to manifest through the medium of their words."

Dogmatic Constitution on Divine Revelation (#12)

"Only the light of faith and meditation on the Word of God can enable us to find everywhere and always the God 'in whom we live and exist' (Acts 17:28); only thus can we seek his will in everything, see Christ in all men, acquaintance or stranger, make sound judgments on the true meaning and value of temporal realities both in themselves and in relation to man's end."

Decree on the Apostolate of Lay People (#4)

Exploring the Sunday Gospel is a structured opportunity for small groups of Christians to break open the Word of God, to understand its rich depth, and to discern how the Word is and can be made manifest in the world. It is an opportunity to gather as one, in the name of Jesus, and pray with that week's gospel: "For where two or three are gathered together in my name, there am I in the midst of them" (Matthew 18:20).

BASIC GUIDELINES

Select an appropriate hour on a regular weekly basis. Consider this hour a priority. It is an occasion for God's grace. It should be unhurried and prayerful. "But as for the seed that fell on rich soil, they are the ones who, when they have heard the word, embrace it with a generous and good heart, and bear fruit through perseverance" (Luke 8:15).

Time and place for gathering can vary according to the needs of the group. Participants should bring their own Bible, their own preferred translation. A variety of translations will broaden discussion.

Because facilitating the group takes no preparation, someone should be invited (or volunteer) to facilitate each week. Be sure everyone who wishes to facilitate is given the opportunity.

Simple refreshments add to a sense of communion.

THE FORMAT

Each week opens with a prayer: "We Gather in Prayer." You will notice that the prayer reflects the theme of the gospel for that week. You will also notice that the prayer is incomplete. Allow those in the group to expand the prayer according to individual, community, and global needs.

After the gathering prayer, the facilitator reads all or part of the gospel for that week ("Read...") and asks someone to read the reflection that follows ("Reflect"). The reflection rephrases the reading and expands on the theme.

The facilitator then leads the group in considering two questions ("Consider") that are designed to break open the Word beyond what the reading and reflection offer. There are no right or wrong responses to these questions. Their purpose is to help the group mine the full richness of the Word.

Next, the facilitator slowly and reverently invites the group into personal petitions ("Let Us Pray"). The list provided reflects the theme of the reading. The last petition allows each person in the group to focus on specific needs (shared with the group or held silently before the Lord). Before the petitions are shared, the group should decide on a common response: "Lord, hear our prayer," "Graciously hear us, O Lord," or any response the group feels is appropriate.

The period of reflective silence ("A Reflective Moment of Silence") offers the group a time for deep intimacy with God. This period may feel awkward at first. With time, however, it will become natural. The facilitator should judge when it's time to invite the group for refreshments (if provided) and further activities or discussions ("Additional Activities/Discussion").

The group may wish to place a picture of Jesus or a crucifix on a table in the center of the gathering. Flowers, in season, even artificial flowers, add to the atmosphere. A lighted candle enhances the environment as well. These and other details help create a mood conducive to prayer and reflection.

GROWING IN FAITH

Maturity and growth take time. We notice the beauty of trees and shrubs and flowers, but we do not see them grow. Only after weeks and months do we perceive their cycle of life.

The Season of
ADVENT

First Sunday of
ADVENT

"...your redemption is at hand."
Luke 21:28

WE GATHER IN PRAYER

Lord, our true home is in heaven with you. You have created us and blessed us with life because you wish to share your love.

You have loved us first. We wish to respond in love to all your gifts and graces. During these weeks of Advent, inspire us to keep in perspective the reason for existence...

Amen

READ LUKE 21:25-28, 34-36

REFLECT

Obviously, Jesus is talking about the end of the world. This world that we live in is not destined to last forever. It had a beginning; it will have an ending. No one, however, really knows how or when that will happen.

According to Jesus, there will be some telltale signs, earthshaking events. Death is not the end of all things, but there will be some form of "judgment."

Advent, the season that leads up to Christmas, is a time to prepare for Christ. We do well to hold our hearts always ready for the coming of the Son of Man.

CONSIDER

- Why is this Scripture read on the First Sunday of Advent?
- What form of judgment might Jesus be referring to?

LET US PRAY

- For all of us here, especially for our spiritual needs
- For those who have forgotten that Christmas is Christ's birthday
- For the grace to celebrate the sacrament of reconciliation with joy and confident peace
- For an increase in the virtues of thoughtfulness and generosity throughout the world
- For our own personal intentions (shared with the group or held silently before the Lord)

A REFLECTIVE MOMENT OF SILENCE

ADDITIONAL ACTIVITIES/DISCUSSION

- How can we make our "decorating" this season reflect an anticipation for Christ's Coming?
- How can we focus more on the true meaning of Advent?

Second Sunday of

ADVENT

...the word of God came to John...
Luke 3:2

WE GATHER IN PRAYER

Lord, when John the Baptist preached to the people along the Jordan River, he encouraged them to be sorry for their sins. He said that this was the proper way to prepare for the coming of the long-awaited Messiah.

Bless our group and our families so that John's words may be as meaningful to us today as they were so long ago.

Give us good hearts. Send the grace we need to be sorry for our sins and to correct our mistakes in good human relations...

Amen

READ LUKE 3:1-6

REFLECT

John might be called the "voice of Advent." His voice seems to echo through the chamber of time to this very day. The Church chooses gospel selections about John at this time of the year because we, today, continue to prepare a way for the Messiah.

Imagine John, a fearless figure, preaching to men and women along the river. He explains that true preparation has to do with reformation of lives. People have to change their ways.

Actually, the Messiah had arrived: Jesus.

CONSIDER

- Is it still necessary to have a change of heart in preparing for Jesus? Why or why not?
- How can we "make straight his paths" as John expressed it? Does it mean "straighten up" or "get your act together," as we would say today?

LET US PRAY

- For those of us who are uncomfortable celebrating the sacrament of reconciliation
- For a greater appreciation of God's forgiveness
- For a true interior preparation for the coming feast of our Lord's nativity
- For insight into the plight of the poor
- For our own personal intentions (shared with the group or held silently before the Lord)

A REFLECTIVE MOMENT OF SILENCE

ADDITIONAL ACTIVITIES/DISCUSSION

- Can our group gather food, clothes, or toys for special people this season?
- Let's discuss the different kinds of poverty.

Third Sunday of
ADVENT

"What then should we do?"
Luke 3:10

WE GATHER IN PRAYER

Lord, make our hearts pleasing to you. Whatever is not in harmony with your holy will, help us change. Just as John the Baptist preached and moved his listeners to repentance, we wish to be sorry for our sins.

Bless us with your peace. Make us cheerful. Make us confident... **Amen**

READ LUKE 3:10-18

REFLECT

Those who took to heart John's preaching want to know specifically what they should do. His message, basically, is that they should be kind, generous, loving, fair, and honest. Apparently, John is such an impressive and powerful speaker that the crowd thinks he might be the expected Messiah. John assures them that one was coming "mightier than I" (3:16).

CONSIDER

- Is there a need for John's kind of preaching today? Why or why not?
- How does this gospel reading fit into the theme of "preparing for Christmas"?

LET US PRAY

- For those who find little joy during the Christmas season
- For our families, that they may be blessed with grace during this Advent season
- For the poor, especially the lonely
- For those who have never known the peace of Jesus, that they may learn of him during these pre-Christmas days
- For our own personal intentions (shared with the group or held silently before the Lord)

A REFLECTIVE MOMENT OF SILENCE

ADDITIONAL ACTIVITIES/DISCUSSION

- What do we know about how Christmas is celebrated in other cultures?
- Let's compose a simple examination of conscience.

Fourth Sunday of

ADVENT

...the infant leaped in her womb...
Luke 1:41

WE GATHER IN PRAYER

Lord, according to your wonderful plan, each of us was conceived within our mother's womb. Jesus, too, was conceived within the womb of Mary, his mother, although through the power and blessing of the Holy Spirit.

Mary looked forward to celebrating the birth of her child. She was full of expectation and excitement.

We, too, want to be full of expectation and excitement. While there was no room in the inn when Jesus was born, we ask you to help us make room in our hearts...

Amen

READ LUKE 1:39-45

REFLECT

When Mary journeys from Nazareth to Elizabeth's town of Ain Karim, she is greeted with tremendous joy. Elizabeth exclaims the words we pray in the Hail Mary: "Blessed are you among women, and blessed is the fruit of your womb" (1:42).

The women are happy to see each other. They rejoice in their pregnancies, their great and blessed expectations. The baby in Elizabeth's womb leaps for joy as well.

CONSIDER

■ What fears or misgivings might Mary or Elizabeth share while they visited together?

■ Why is this a fitting Scripture for the last Sunday before Christmas?

LET US PRAY

■ For a true and deep appreciation of the Incarnation
■ For all pregnant women
■ For a great respect for God's gift of human life, from womb to tomb
■ For joy in our families as we do what we can to keep the genuine spirit of Christmas foremost in our hearts
■ For our own personal intentions (shared with the group or held silently before the Lord)

A REFLECTIVE MOMENT OF SILENCE

ADDITIONAL ACTIVITIES/DISCUSSION

■ Discuss the rigors a woman of Mary's culture had to face in making a long journey.
■ Would parents today discuss the same things that Mary and Elizabeth discussed?

The Season of
CHRISTMAS

CHRISTMAS DAY

...the light shines in the darkness...
John 1:5

WE GATHER IN PRAYER

Lord, there was great joy in the hearts of Mary and Joseph at the birth of their child. They were a family, a holy family. They were intent on doing your holy will. They tried to please you in all things.

Bless our group and our families with joy. May we welcome all visitors to our homes with the same joy that Mary and Joseph welcomed Jesus. What we do for one another, Lord, we do for you...

Amen

READ JOHN 1:1-18

REFLECT

John writes in a different way than Matthew, Mark, and Luke. John's approach seems more philosophical. He says, "...the Word became flesh" (1:14).

God just said the Word and it was done. God said, "Let there be light and water and earth," and all came into existence. When it came time for Jesus to enter our world, God simply said the Word and it happened. Mary conceived.

Christmas is the day we celebrate this in-breaking of God into our midst.

CONSIDER

■ Why did the Church choose this gospel selection for Christmas day?

■ How do our lives reflect our belief in Jesus Christ?

LET US PRAY

■ For the peace that only God can give

■ For everyone who has not heard of Christ

■ For a true understanding of what it means to be more blessed in giving than in receiving

■ For a true appreciation of all our blessings

■ For our own personal intentions (shared with the group or held silently before the Lord)

A REFLECTIVE MOMENT OF SILENCE

ADDITIONAL ACTIVITIES/DISCUSSION

■ Let's read and discuss the gospel readings for other Masses for Christmas (Luke 2:1-14 and 2:15-20).

■ As a small Christian community celebrating the birth of Christ, let's share a special treat.

(Sunday in the Octave of Christmas)
HOLY FAMILY

"Why were you looking for me?"
Luke 2:49

WE GATHER IN PRAYER

Lord, bless our group and our families; guide us all in wisdom and truth.

Nothing stands still in life. Life means change. May each day bring a change into our lives that we can recognize as growth. Help us accept your grace and wisdom in seeking your holy will...

Amen

READ LUKE 2:41-52

REFLECT

Understandably, Joseph and Mary assume that Jesus is with relatives or friends in the caravan returning to Nazareth. Once they realize he isn't, they backtrack to Jerusalem. They surely do not comprehend Jesus' answer when they find him in the Temple talking with the learned men.

Jesus asks Mary and Joseph if they understand that he has to be in his Father's house. Jesus is not disobedient. He is simply doing something that is a bit beyond his parents' expectations and comprehension.

There are no other details or incidents of Jesus' childhood in the gospels.

CONSIDER
- How might we interpret this unusual gospel passage?
- Why is this a significant story from Jesus' childhood?

LET US PRAY
- For all parents
- For all children
- For all those who teach children
- For families who have special challenges
- For our own personal intentions (shared with the group or held silently before the Lord)

A REFLECTIVE MOMENT OF SILENCE

ADDITIONAL ACTIVITIES/DISCUSSION
- Let's find out more about whom Luke was addressing when he wrote his account of Jesus' life.
- How would we react today if one of our children responded the way Jesus did to his parents?

Octave of Christmas (New Year's Day)

MARY, MOTHER OF GOD

...reflecting on them in her heart.
Luke 2:19

WE GATHER IN PRAYER

Lord, we honor Mary because you chose her to be the mother of your Son. You made a choice that was without flaw. No other person could better fulfill your divine design. Mary was full of love, goodness, and grace.

Help us become the persons you wish us to be. May we faithfully offer a resounding "Yes" when your will is conveyed...

Amen

READ LUKE 2:16-21

REFLECT

This is a brief gospel reading. The shepherds arrive at the site of Jesus' birth and recount their experience of the angels' announcement in the fields: "For today in the city of David a savior has been born for you who is Messiah and Lord" (2:11). Mary and Joseph are amazed at what the shepherds say.

We are told that "Mary kept all these things, reflecting on them in her heart" (2:19). Imagine your child's birth being announced by angels to people in outlying areas.

Mary is called the Mother of God. She remained faithful to God's invitation to participate in the salvation of the world. She is the channel through which God came into the world and remains a channel of wisdom and peace for us today.

CONSIDER

- What does the title "Mother of God" mean?
- What role does Mary play in the Church today?

LET US PRAY

- For newborn babies
- For the parents of newborn babies, that they will dedicate themselves to God's invitation to the vocation of parenthood
- For all parents as they struggle to provide spiritual leadership in the home
- For those who have not yet learned of Jesus, Messiah and Lord
- For our own personal intentions (shared with the group or held silently before the Lord)

A REFLECTIVE MOMENT OF SILENCE

ADDITIONAL ACTIVITIES/DISCUSSION

- Let's share stories from our own lives about God's overwhelming nearness in "announcing" something remarkable.
- How valuable is the rosary as a means of prayer?

Second Sunday After
CHRISTMAS

The true light, which enlightens everyone...
John 1:9

WE GATHER IN PRAYER

Lord, we know you through Jesus, your Son. John the Evangelist tells us that no one has seen you, our Father, but that Jesus has made you known. Jesus declares that if we know him, we know you.

Help us as a group, and help our families, understand and appreciate that you became one of us: God became man. Move our hearts to accept this revelation as a matter of great love and not mere information...

Amen

READ JOHN 1:1-18

REFLECT

If this gospel sounds familiar, it is. This is the same passage proclaimed on Christmas day.

This gospel was written many years after Jesus' death, resurrection, and ascension. By the time this was written, the early Christians were familiar with the gospels of Matthew, Mark, and Luke. Nonetheless, John makes a great contribution to the faith in this writing. Throughout his gospel, John emphasizes the themes of life, light, truth, and the preexistence of Jesus Christ.

Notice how John refers to Jesus as enlightening every person who comes into the world.

CONSIDER
- How does Jesus enlighten everyone who comes into the world?
- What does John mean when he says "...while the law was given through Moses, grace and truth came through Jesus Christ" (1:17)?

LET US PRAY
- For a deeper appreciation of Jesus' true presence in the Eucharist
- For good hearts and Spirit-filled dispositions
- For all missionaries around the globe
- For the wisdom to cherish revelation
- For our own personal intentions (shared with the group or held silently before the Lord)

A REFLECTIVE MOMENT OF SILENCE

ADDITIONAL ACTIVITIES/DISCUSSION
- How are we still celebrating the birth of Christ?
- How are we different from others who have never heard of Jesus Christ...or are we?

EPIPHANY

"Where is the newborn..."
Matthew 2:2

WE GATHER IN PRAYER

Lord, the wise men came to honor Jesus with gifts. They were intent on giving rather than receiving.

Form our minds and hearts to see how good and right it is to have this intention, especially when we attend Mass. We want to honor and worship you, to give you the glory that your Son offers in the sacrifice of his entire life...

Amen

READ MATTHEW 2:1-12

REFLECT

The wise men are not Jews; they are foreigners, strangers. Yet, God gives them a special role in salvation history.

Epiphany, a Greek word meaning "showing" or "manifest," is God's worldwide announcement of his Son to the world. The wise men travel through Jerusalem and, unknowingly, alert Herod about the birth of the Messiah. Steadily, they move on to Bethlehem, where they reverently and humbly offer their priceless gifts to the Infant. The world sees for itself that, indeed, this child is destined for greatness in the eyes of God.

CONSIDER

- What significance do the wise men play in identifying this child as the Messiah?
- Why are there parallels between this story and the story of the birth of Moses? (See Exodus 1:15–2:10.)

LET US PRAY

- For all of us who fear God, that we may learn to trust the meek and humble heart of Jesus
- For the leaders of all nations, that they may have the good of their people at heart, especially the poor and homeless
- For all of us who struggle with our faith, that we will be renewed in God's grace
- For the courage to live by our convictions
- For our own personal intentions (shared with the group or held silently before the Lord)

A REFLECTIVE MOMENT OF SILENCE

ADDITIONAL ACTIVITIES/DISCUSSION

- How can we celebrate this feast in our families?
- When have we found the goodness of Christ in an unlikely place, person, event?

BAPTISM OF THE LORD

...heaven was opened...
Luke 3:21

WE GATHER IN PRAYER

Lord, baptism is not just a social ceremony; it is a tremendous statement of faith and the beginning of a lifelong commitment. Baptism bonds our relationship with you. You extend your love and mercy to us—and we open ourselves to say "Yes."

Help us appreciate the meaning of baptism. Help us understand that our own baptism was not a long-ago and long-forgotten moment in time but a moment in time that still reflects your unconditional love...

Amen

READ LUKE 3:15-16, 21-22

REFLECT

John the Baptist preaches repentance along the Jordan River. There is excitement in the air as he attracts people from all over the countryside. Some of these people think that John might be the Messiah, but he quickly corrects them: "...one mightier than I is coming" (3:16). John says that this mightier one will "...baptize you with the holy Spirit and fire" (3:16).

The baptism of Jesus marks the beginning of his public ministry. When John baptizes Jesus, Jesus represents all sinners. Later, Jesus suffers and dies on the cross for all the sins and sinners of the world.

CONSIDER

- Why does God speak at the baptism of Jesus?
- Do the people who witness this event understand its significance? Why or why not?

LET US PRAY

- For the conversion of all people preparing to celebrate baptism
- For parents who have just had their child baptized
- For the blessings of Christ's forgiveness in all things
- For the grace to follow Jesus in our daily lives
- For our own personal intentions (shared with the group or held silently before the Lord)

A REFLECTIVE MOMENT OF SILENCE

ADDITIONAL ACTIVITIES/DISCUSSION

- What is the general attitude toward baptism today?
- What "beginnings" do we remember—beginnings that we didn't know were "beginnings" at the time?

The Season of
LENT

First Sunday in
LENT

...into the desert...
Luke 4:1

WE GATHER IN PRAYER

Dear God, "lead us not into temptation." When we are faced with an occasion of possible sin, pull us to yourself.

Remind us of Jesus' temptations in the desert and his strength to desire only you.

Teach us the ways of self-discipline and invite us into intimate prayer...

Amen

READ LUKE 4:1-13

REFLECT

The devil tempts Jesus to see how committed he is to his Father. First, the devil tries to play on Jesus' hunger: a universal human weakness. Even in his weakened state, however, Jesus chooses fidelity to his Father. He knows that his hunger for his Father is far more savage than his hunger for food.

Next, the devil turns to the all-time human weakness for power and prestige: "I shall give to you all this power and their glory" (4:6). But Jesus knows his identity: servant. Power and prestige are not the will of his Father; love and service are.

Finally, the devil tries to tempt Jesus with pain-free living. But Jesus knows that the journey to his Father is a journey of pain. He is willing to take every step of that journey.

CONSIDER
- Why is this gospel appropriate for the beginning of Lent?
- What does this gospel tell us about the humanity of Jesus?

LET US PRAY
- For a rich Lent, that we may better value the struggles and joys of the Christian life
- For trust in God when we are tempted
- For patience, despite physical and moral trials
- For those of us who suffer from the perils of apathy and indifference
- For our own personal intentions (shared with the group or held silently before the Lord)

A REFLECTIVE MOMENT OF SILENCE

ADDITIONAL ACTIVITIES/DISCUSSION
- Let's identify these same temptations in our lives today.
- What good are temptations?

Second Sunday in

LENT

...up the mountain...
Luke 9:28

WE GATHER IN PRAYER

Lord, encourage us as Jesus encouraged his friends Peter, James, and John. We need their same faith and trust.

May we glow with the same splendor Jesus did, knowing we are loved passionately and unconditionally. Make our hearts light as we tread the days of Lent, as we anticipate the joy of Easter morning...

Amen

READ LUKE 9:28-36

REFLECT

Jesus takes three of his friends to the top of the mountain to pray. As Jesus enters prayer, his friends doze off. When they awake, they find Jesus in their midst, aglow and talking with Moses and Elijah.

Immediately, Peter wants to hang on to the moment; he wants to build tents and settle in for a while. But God has other plans.

A cloud descends over the group, and a voice proclaims, "This is my chosen Son..." (9:35). When the cloud recedes, Jesus is alone.

CONSIDER
- What significance does this gospel have for the season of Lent?
- Peter's response is "...let us make three tents..." (9:33). What does his response say about the Christian journey?

LET US PRAY
- For all those who suffer physical, emotional, and spiritual pain
- For our own timidity, that we may be blessed with patience and perseverance
- For the wisdom to welcome our own transforming moments
- For the courage to make our transforming moments opportunities for witnessing to the goodness of God
- For our own personal intentions (shared with the group or held silently before the Lord)

A REFLECTIVE MOMENT OF SILENCE

ADDITIONAL ACTIVITIES/DISCUSSION
- How does this gospel support our faith?
- What would it take to transfigure us?

Third Sunday in

LENT

"...in search of fruit..."
Luke 13:6

WE GATHER IN PRAYER

Dear God, we are sinners and are in need of repentance and your mercy. We are sorry, honestly and deeply sorry.

As the weeks of Lent unfold, teach us to take inventory of our spiritual lives. Give us the goodwill to be sorry for our willful mistakes...

Amen

READ LUKE 13:1-9

REFLECT

Jesus uses national catastrophes to support his teachings. He tries to get his listeners to understand that the victims of disaster are not guilty of some atrocity and therefore ruination befalls them.

Jesus draws the attention of his listeners into their own hearts. He speaks of the need for repentance. He calls for a change of mind and heart, a reversal of direction. He challenges his listeners to deliberate thought, word, and deed.

CONSIDER

- What is the meaning of the parable about the fig tree?
- Why is it appropriate for the parable about the fig tree to follow Jesus' words about repentance?

LET US PRAY

- For the strength to continue with our good Lenten resolutions
- For the grace of repentance when our hearts turn hard with self-righteousness
- For the peace of a good confession during this season of Lent
- For hearts brimming with compassion
- For our own personal intentions (shared with the group or held silently before the Lord)

A REFLECTIVE MOMENT OF SILENCE

ADDITIONAL ACTIVITIES/DISCUSSION

- "Well, she/he had it coming." Why do we say this, and is it true?
- What local, national, and international tragedies have we been responsible for as individuals, as a group, and as a society?

Fourth Sunday in
LENT

"...the celebration began..."
Luke 15:24

WE GATHER IN PRAYER

Lord, hear our pleas for our own conversions and the conversions of all people everywhere. Release our hearts from judgmentalism to love unconditionally as you do.

Guide us through the mysteries of repentance, compassion, and mercy...

Amen

READ LUKE 15:1-3, 11-32

REFLECT

The scribes and Pharisees complain that Jesus associates with sinners. They do not know that Jesus relates with others out of a judgment-free system. He loves the person without reference to what the person does. Little do the scribes and Pharisees realize that Jesus, in fact, loves them!

Jesus tells the story about two sons who make different choices in life. The one son ends up desperate, regretting his choices; the other son ends up angry, regretting his choices.

CONSIDER

- How were both sons in the parable "lost"?
- In one sentence, summarize Jesus' purpose in telling this parable.

LET US PRAY

- For all young people as they make their choices in life
- For parents, that they may persevere in patience with their children
- For ourselves, that our hearts will be stripped of judgmentalism and we can love freely
- For those of us in the process of making major decisions, that our choices are guided by the wisdom of the Spirit
- For our own personal intentions (shared with the group or held silently before the Lord)

A REFLECTIVE MOMENT OF SILENCE

ADDITIONAL ACTIVITIES/DISCUSSION

- What part of us is the father in the parable? the "wayward" son? the "loyal" son?
- Do we sometimes get angry when we do what is responsible, moral, Christian? Why?

Fifth Sunday in

"So what do you say?"
John 8:5

WE GATHER IN PRAYER

Lord, write the Spirit of the Law in our hearts. Turn our attention away from sin and toward forgiveness. Fill our hearts with a ready acceptance of ourselves and others, broken and imperfect.

We follow you through these days of Lent, Lord, to Jerusalem...

Amen

READ JOHN 8:1-11

REFLECT

The time of Jesus' death is quickly approaching. He spends his nights on the Mount of Olives and his days in the Temple. The people flock to hear him teach.

In the midst of one such assembly, the scribes and the Pharisees show up with a woman they accuse of committing adultery. The Mosaic Law called for the death of both partners in the sin of adultery. We can't help but note that the woman's partner is mysteriously absent.

The scribes and Pharisees think they have Jesus trapped on this one. If Jesus allows the woman to be stoned, obviously he is not a man of mercy; if he allows the woman to go free, he defies the sacred Jewish law.

Rather than entering into the game of you-win-I-lose, Jesus blows the scene apart by turning the accusers around to look at themselves: "Let the one among you who is without sin be the first to throw a stone at her" (8:7).

CONSIDER

- Why is this gospel significant at this point in Jesus' life?
- What good qualities are exhibited by the woman's accusers?

LET US PRAY

- For the humility to recognize our own sinfulness
- For goodness of heart, that we can forgive ourselves and others
- For our families, that they learn to accept rather than judge
- For those who work in our judicial system, that they will allow the spirit of the law to direct their efforts
- For our own personal intentions (shared with the group or held silently before the Lord)

A REFLECTIVE MOMENT OF SILENCE

ADDITIONAL ACTIVITIES/DISCUSSION

- Discuss the following statement: "Everyone deserves justice; no one deserves mercy."
- Should we forgive and forget? Why or why not?

(Palm Sunday)
PASSION SUNDAY

...he breathed his last...
Luke 23:46

WE GATHER IN PRAYER

Dear Lord, we walk the Way of the Cross with you and one another during this final week of Lent. Help us feel your rejection, your fear, your pain—your love.

Bless us with a sincere appreciation for the mystery of your death. May our hearts be profoundly moved to slip our shoulders under the cross, next to yours...

Amen

READ LUKE 23:26-49

REFLECT

Jesus' cross is crushing. He's been up all night, tormented and teased, and now the weight of the cross digs into his bruised flesh.

Jesus encounters many folks during these last hours of his life: Simon, a large crowd, a group of women, the two criminals who are executed with him. Somehow, the lives of these people are deeply affected by their encounter with the Son of God on the way to his execution.

CONSIDER

- How does this gospel bring us closer to Jesus our Savior?
- What made the centurion conclude, "This man was innocent beyond doubt" (23:47)?

LET US PRAY

- For a greater appreciation of God's boundless love
- For a firm resolution to bear our crosses with enduring patience
- For the charity and courage to be Simon to others as we help them carry their crosses
- For the wisdom to know if the crosses on our shoulders are genuine or products of self-abuse
- For our own personal intentions (shared with the group or held silently before the Lord)

A REFLECTIVE MOMENT OF SILENCE

ADDITIONAL ACTIVITIES/DISCUSSION

- Why remember pain?
- How do we bear our own crosses and contribute to the weight of others at the same time?

The Season of EASTER

EASTER SUNDAY

...he had to rise...
John 20:9

WE GATHER IN PRAYER

Lord, fill our hearts with wonder and joy as we contemplate the empty tomb. Help us make room in our lives for the mystery of this splendid event.

May we be watchful for your presence in our lives. May we rejoice with the true meaning of the Resurrection and come to appreciate what it means in our lives...

Amen

READ JOHN 20:1-9

REFLECT

The morning is breaking and Mary of Magdala is at the tomb. When she realizes, however, that the tomb is empty, she runs to tell Peter and "the other disciple whom Jesus loved." They are incredulous, of course, and simply have to see for themselves. With fear, frustration, anticipation, and confusion, the two men run to the tomb only to find, just as Mary had said, an empty tomb.

Peter enters the tomb and makes careful note of the burial cloths. The other disciple, however, enters the tomb and "he saw and believed" (20:8).

CONSIDER

- What is the significance of the difference between Peter's response to the empty tomb and the disciple's response?
- What is the significance of this event to our faith?

LET US PRAY

- For genuine Christian joy as we celebrate Jesus' Resurrection
- For a joyful spirit as we gather in community to celebrate this central mystery of our faith
- For a peaceful heart in the face of profound mystery
- For all those who wait, clinging to hope in the face of total despair
- For our own personal intentions (shared with the group or held silently before the Lord)

A REFLECTIVE MOMENT OF SILENCE

ADDITIONAL ACTIVITIES/DISCUSSION

- How have the past six weeks of Lent prepared us to celebrate the Resurrection with greater faith?
- Let's review the things we do and the symbols we use to celebrate Easter to see if we are, in fact, focused on the risen Lord.

Second Sunday of
EASTER

"I will not believe."
John 20:25

WE GATHER IN PRAYER

Oh, Lord, bless our unbelief. Quiet our doubts and fill us with the faith of the apostles. When you appear in our midst as the unemployed, the fearful child, the grieving friend, the pesky neighbor, fill our hearts with loyal faith.

May Thomas' prayer be ever on our lips: "My Lord and my God!" (20:28)...

Amen

READ JOHN 20:19-31

REFLECT

What a state of fear and confusion the apostles are in as they huddle behind locked doors late at night. That very morning they had found the body of their beloved friend, Jesus, missing from the tomb. What are they to make of that? Has someone taken Jesus' body? If so, why? Do the Romans think *they* stole the body? Are their lives in danger?

Then, despite locked doors, Jesus appears offering them peace. Knowing the apostles would struggle with believing their own eyes, Jesus shows them his pierced hands and side. What rejoicing there is in the group.

But Thomas misses out. When he does show up, he adamantly refuses to believe the apostles. "Unless I see the mark of the nails in his hands and put my finger into the nailmarks and put my hand into his side, I will not believe" (20:25).

CONSIDER
■ Why did Thomas exclaim, "My Lord and my God!" (20:28)?
■ How is Thomas actually a brave and faithful apostle?

LET US PRAY
■ For an increase in our own faith
■ For those recently baptized, confirmed, and welcomed into the faith
■ For all those who have never heard the Good News
■ For all those who are persecuted and oppressed for their faith in Jesus Christ
■ For our own personal intentions (shared with the group or held silently before the Lord)

A REFLECTIVE MOMENT OF SILENCE

ADDITIONAL ACTIVITIES/DISCUSSION
■ What is the symbolic significance of bodily wounds and scars?
■ How can we believe in the risen Lord without seeing him for ourselves?

Third Sunday of
EASTER

"...you know everything..."
John 21:17

WE GATHER IN PRAYER

Lord, when our hearts hear you ask "Do you love me?" we want to answer with a resounding "Yes, yes, yes!" Yet, we are weak. We trust that you will never cease to ask—and that we will never cease to answer "Yes!"

May we listen for your direction and respond as the apostles did when you told them to cast their nets...

Amen

READ JOHN 21:1-19

REFLECT

Fishing was not a casual pastime for these men; fishing was their livelihood. This particular band of men had been fishing all night and were returning without a catch.

From the shore, a stranger calls to them, "Cast the net over the right side of the boat..." (21:6). Immediately, the net is full to the breaking point—although it does not break.

In this moment, the men begin to realize that the stranger on the shore is Jesus. In a short while, Jesus invites the men to breakfast. "And none of the disciples dared to ask him, 'Who are you?' because they realized it was the Lord" (21:12).

It seems, however, that Jesus has a particular issue with Peter; he seems to want to emphasize something. Not once, not twice, but three times he asks Peter if he loves him.

CONSIDER

■ Why does Jesus say something different after each of Peter's responses to "Do you love me?" (21:15, 16, 17)

■ What is the significance of this event in the ongoing account of the Resurrection?

LET US PRAY

■ For the pope and all bishops around the world

■ For all baptized Christians, that we may be in solidarity with the teaching of Christ

■ For the courage to respond to Jesus' invitation to "Follow me"

■ For all those who weary with the toil of work they find neither satisfying nor productive

■ For our own personal intentions (shared with the group or held silently before the Lord)

A REFLECTIVE MOMENT OF SILENCE

ADDITIONAL ACTIVITIES/DISCUSSION

■ Why does it seem impolite to ask "Do you love me?"

■ Let's find out how Peter died and see how it aligns with this gospel.

Fourth Sunday of
EASTER

"...I know them..."
John 10:27

WE GATHER IN PRAYER

Lord, plant in our hearts an appreciation for the promises of eternal life that Jesus offered. Teach us to follow Jesus, our eternal Shepherd, and to respond to the sound of his voice wherever and whenever we hear it.

Lead us in ways everlasting. Let us not be led astray...

Amen

READ JOHN 10:27-30

REFLECT

The verses preceding this reading tell us that Jesus is wandering around the Temple area during the feast of the Dedication, an eight-day festival of lights (Hanukkah). As usual, a crowd gathers. This particular group wants Jesus, once and for all, to proclaim himself the Messiah—or not. They want something definite.

Jesus' response is clear: "I told you and you do not believe" (10:25). Using the image of a shepherd, not a highly respected figure in that day and culture, Jesus explains that they wouldn't have to insist on something definite if they were, in fact, of his flock.

CONSIDER

- What does Jesus mean when he says, "...I know them..." (10:27)?
- What do these few lines say about eternal life?

LET US PRAY

- For alert hearts, that we will know the voice of our Savior when we hear it
- For the grace of a happy death
- For a great confidence in the loving care of the Good Shepherd
- For strength and confidence, that we will witness to our faith in Christ at home, school, in the workplace, in the neighborhood
- For our own personal intentions (shared with the group or held silently before the Lord)

A REFLECTIVE MOMENT OF SILENCE

ADDITIONAL ACTIVITIES/DISCUSSION

- Let's discuss our images of heaven.
- Do we need proof that Jesus is God's Son, the promised Messiah? If so, why? If not, why?

Fifth Sunday of
EASTER

"...only a little while longer..."
John 13:33

WE GATHER IN PRAYER

Lord, make us glow with the distinguishing characteristic of Christians: love. Plant this philosophy of life deep within our souls so that all who encounter us will know our truest identity as Christians.

Bless the world with this same love. May your patience, kindness, and justice settle ever deeper into the center of humankind...

Amen

READ JOHN 13:31-35

REFLECT

The scene is the familiar Last Supper. The moment is the exchange between Jesus and his friends following Judas' departure into the night.

Jesus uses this opportunity to alert the apostles to the course of events about to unfold around them. Naturally, they don't understand. Later, recalling Jesus' words, they would understand clearly. Later, after the Resurrection, Ascension, and the moment of Pentecost, the apostles would display the love that would distinguish them as followers of Jesus.

CONSIDER

- Why would Jesus refer to his apostles as "my children" (13:33)?
- What is the significance of these words of Jesus following Judas' departure?

LET US PRAY

- For all those who find it difficult to love because their lives are riddled with fear
- For all those who live in war-torn regions of the world
- For ourselves, that we may have the faith and love of Jesus Christ to the point of death
- For those we find difficult to love
- For our own personal intentions (shared with the group or held silently before the Lord)

A REFLECTIVE MOMENT OF SILENCE

ADDITIONAL ACTIVITIES/DISCUSSION

- Let's ask ourselves: "Are we known as Christians because our love for others is evident or because we go to church and are basically good people?"
- How do love and justice seem to compete against each other at times?

Sixth Sunday of EASTER

"...he will teach you everything..."
John 14:26

WE GATHER IN PRAYER

Lord, plant in each of us a loyal heart. May we hear your word clearly and keep it with steady faith.

Open our eyes to see you in our midst, to experience your presence in those around us...

Amen

READ JOHN 14:23-29

REFLECT

Jesus is about to face his trial, torture, and death. He is trying to share all his wisdom and peace with the apostles; they're going to need it.

Jesus knows how disturbed his friends are going to be. He knows he's become a leader in their midst, someone they trust and believe in. When he's gone, he wants them to remember him and to realize that he is, in fact, still with them. Jesus wants to plant the seed of peace in the hearts of his apostles.

CONSIDER

■ What does Jesus mean when he says, "Not as the world gives do I give it to you" (14:27)?
■ How do Jesus' words reassure the apostles?

LET US PRAY

■ For open minds and hearts, that we may claim the peace and wisdom of the Holy Spirit
■ For a greater understanding of God's ways
■ For fidelity to God's commandments
■ For a perfect trust in the presence of Jesus in our midst, that we may overcome fear and anxiety
■ For our own personal intentions (shared with the group or held silently before the Lord)

A REFLECTIVE MOMENT OF SILENCE

ADDITIONAL ACTIVITIES/DISCUSSION

■ How is our love and loyalty to God challenged in everyday life?
■ Let's share stories about times when we felt the presence of Jesus very close at hand.

ASCENSION OF THE LORD

...he parted from them...
Luke 24:51

WE GATHER IN PRAYER

Dear God, we want to take up the mission of Jesus and make it our own. We want to give witness to all that Jesus is.

Empower us with the courage of the Holy Spirit. Clothe us in the power "from on high" (24:49) that Jesus promised to all his followers...

Amen

READ LUKE 24:46-53

REFLECT

Jesus is about to leave his apostles. He reminds them to believe what they see and to trust what they know in their hearts. He emphasizes the forgiveness of sins. He promises them a special power that will be their guide and strength through the days and years ahead. Finally, he blesses the apostles and is gone from them.

Notice that the apostles do not mourn and linger. They give praise and then return to the city with much rejoicing. Already, they are beginning to get the idea.

CONSIDER

- How does this account serve as a close to Jesus' mission here on earth?
- In light of what we know about the power of the Holy Spirit, why did Jesus have to part from his apostles and the world?

LET US PRAY

- For the Church, that all the baptized will give witness to Christ
- For a personal frame of mind that enables us to hold the cares of this world in our hearts
- For the gift of understanding, that we can fathom the events of Christ's life
- For the gift of understanding, that we can fathom the events of our own lives
- For our own personal intentions (shared with the group or held silently before the Lord)

A REFLECTIVE MOMENT OF SILENCE

ADDITIONAL ACTIVITIES/DISCUSSION

- How are endings always beginnings?
- How do we experience ourselves as "clothed with power from on high" (24:49)?

Seventh Sunday of
EASTER

"...that the world may believe..."
John 17:21

WE GATHER IN PRAYER

Lord, let there be unity and harmony among all people. This was Jesus' prayer, and it is our prayer. Jesus prayed for oneness in mind and heart among followers; today, we do the same.

We ask to know you better, to serve you through service to others, and to follow your Word always...

Amen

READ JOHN 17:20-26

REFLECT

This reading is intense; we can feel the passionate love of Jesus for both his Father and all humankind. He wants the world to know that love, to know his Father, to know him. He is appreciative of all those who have followed him: "Father, they are your gift to me" (17:24).

Primarily, Jesus prays for unity and community. He knows that the genuine love of God will be reflected to the world only in the peaceful harmony that humankind nurtures and shares.

CONSIDER

- Why is the account of this event positioned right before Jesus' arrest?
- How can this reading foster harmony?

LET US PRAY

- For all humankind, that the love of God may bring global unity
- For open hearts, that we will appreciate the Truth in all human beings
- For the wisdom to know how to support others on their faith journeys
- For all those who suffer because of their religious beliefs
- For our own personal intentions (shared with the group or held silently before the Lord)

A REFLECTIVE MOMENT OF SILENCE

ADDITIONAL ACTIVITIES/DISCUSSION

- Let's discuss the meaning and importance of ecumenism.
- How do we value our brothers and sisters who are not Christian?

PENTECOST

...the doors were locked...
John 20:19

WE GATHER IN PRAYER

Lord, your power is awesome. Earthquakes, cyclones, and tornadoes put the "fear of God" in us—but they are nothing compared to the power of your Spirit.

Release in us an energy that can break through the barriers of sin. Bless us with the wisdom and courage to take your Spirit into the world with power and authority...

Amen

READ JOHN 20:19-23

REFLECT

We read about this event on the Second Sunday of Easter. Scared, fearing for their lives, Jesus' followers cower away from the public eye. Bringing peace, Jesus appears in their midst.

The significance of this reading on Pentecost points to the power of the Spirit. "...he breathed on them and said to them, 'Receive the holy Spirit...' " (20:22). Often referred to as the birthday of the Church, Pentecost marks the conversion of Jesus' followers. From the shadows of their hiding place, the apostles march into the marketplace declaring the Good News. Afire with the power of the Spirit, they are finally ready for true discipleship.

CONSIDER

- What is the significance of Jesus' first words to the apostles: "Peace be with you" (20:19)?
- Why is this event, instead of the Resurrection, considered the birthday of the Church?

LET US PRAY

- For the continued guidance of the Holy Spirit in the Church
- For inspiration in developing the creative talents of all people
- For an appreciation of the unitive power of the Spirit, a force that brings harmony, not division
- For God's graces upon all those who make decisions that affect the lives of millions
- For our own personal intentions (shared with the group or held silently before the Lord)

A REFLECTIVE MOMENT OF SILENCE

ADDITIONAL ACTIVITIES/DISCUSSION

- How do we experience the fire of the Holy Spirit in our lives today?
- What is the significance of the sacrament of confirmation with relation to the Holy Spirit and Pentecost?

TRINITY SUNDAY

"...he will guide you to all truth..."
John 16:13

WE GATHER IN PRAYER

Lord, increase our faith in you as the one, true God. Claim our total faithfulness in worship. In your goodness, reveal to us that which only the Holy Spirit in us can understand.

May we grow ever wiser in your ways, Lord, more and more willing to speak your Truth to the world...

Amen

READ JOHN 16:12-15

REFLECT

This Scripture comes from part of Jesus' discourse at the Last Supper. He desperately wants the apostles to understand the intimate connection between himself and the Father. He wants them to know the oneness they share with him and how the grace of the Spirit embodies their oneness.

The triangle and the shamrock have long been used as symbols of the Trinity, but they fail to convey the total mystery. After all, the Trinity is not something to be understood; it is to be entered.

CONSIDER

- How does this Scripture passage speak of the Trinity?
- Why couldn't Jesus tell his apostles everything they needed to know?

LET US PRAY

- For all of us as we sincerely seek the Truth, that the Holy Spirit will enlighten us
- For theologians and catechists, that they may find ways to explain the nature of the Holy Trinity while inviting us into the mystery
- For the perseverance to remain faithful to the Three-in-One God
- For the willingness to love all things in the name of the Father, Son, and Holy Spirit
- For our own personal intentions (shared with the group or held silently before the Lord)

A REFLECTIVE MOMENT OF SILENCE

ADDITIONAL ACTIVITIES/DISCUSSION

- What other simple symbols can we use to understand the nature of the Trinity?
- When have we withheld things from our children because we knew they couldn't comprehend? Does this simplify or complicate things?

BODY AND BLOOD OF CHRIST

They all ate and were satisfied.
Luke 9:17

WE GATHER IN PRAYER

Lord, lead us to a passionate love for you in the Eucharist. Open our hearts to understand the oneness and intimacy we have with you in the community of worshipers, the Word, and the breaking and sharing of the bread.

May we reverence you in the Blessed Sacrament...

Amen

READ LUKE 9:11-17

REFLECT

Imagine a crowd of five thousand people. Even by today's standard of high-tech crowd control, five thousand people is a lot to handle, to keep comfortable.

The apostles know this. They encourage Jesus to let the people see to their own needs, to find their own food and lodgings. Jesus, however, is as concerned for five thousand people as he is for one. He challenges the apostles to see their options and to trust that loving attention always merits grand results.

The Church invites us to make the connection between Jesus' miracle of multiplying the loaves and fish to the splendid nourishment of the Eucharist. It is beyond human ability to feed five thousand people with only a few loaves of bread and a couple of fish, yet Jesus does it. In the same way, Jesus nourishes us again and again, by the millions and through the centuries, on his body and blood.

CONSIDER

■ Discuss the options the apostles considered.
■ What is the significance of there being "leftovers" after this feast?

LET US PRAY

■ For a deep devotion to Christ present in the Eucharist
■ For all those preparing to celebrate their first Communion
■ For a better understanding of what the Mass celebrates
■ For those of us who doubt the Real Presence of Christ in the Eucharist
■ For our own personal intentions (shared with the group or held silently before the Lord)

A REFLECTIVE MOMENT OF SILENCE

ADDITIONAL ACTIVITIES/DISCUSSION

■ How has devotion to the Blessed Sacrament changed over the years?
■ How can we celebrate eucharist in our own homes?

The Season of
ORDINARY TIME

Second Sunday in
ORDINARY TIME

...the wine ran short...
John 2:3

WE GATHER IN PRAYER

Lord, our faith has a rich tradition of praying to Mary. At Cana in Galilee, Jesus changed water into wine, a miracle, at Mary's request. It would seem that Mary had only to mention a request to her son, and it was granted.

We recognize the closeness of our blessed Mother and her son. Bless us with the same confidence Mary had in Jesus...

Amen

READ JOHN 2:1-12

REFLECT

According to John, the evangelist who recorded the incident of the wedding at Cana, the changing of water into wine is the first of Jesus' public miracles. There would be many more. Crowds would flock to Jesus for cures and blessings.

It seems insignificant to perform a miracle just because the wedding party runs out of wine. Perhaps it shows how tender and thoughtful Jesus is even in the most common circumstances. Perhaps it shows the degree to which Jesus respects his mother's compassion and mercy.

CONSIDER

- What is Jesus trying to say when he tells his mother, "My hour has not yet come" (2:4)?
- Why is this story significant in the tradition of the Christian faith?

LET US PRAY

- For faithful confidence in Jesus' and Mary's love for us
- For all married couples, that their lives be blessed with the presence of Jesus and Mary
- For all engaged couples, that they have the prayerful intention to lead their lives according to God's will
- For young people who are beginning to date, that they may realize marriage is a holy state
- For our own personal intentions (shared with the group or held silently before the Lord)

A REFLECTIVE MOMENT OF SILENCE

ADDITIONAL ACTIVITIES/DISCUSSION

- Let's discuss the role Mary plays in the Catholic faith.
- Let's invite someone to share his or her pilgrimage to Medjugorje.

Third Sunday in
ORDINARY TIME

He came to Nazareth.
Luke 4:16

WE GATHER IN PRAYER

Lord, rip judgmentalism from our hearts so that we recognize you in our midst. When we hesitate to witness to the unconditional love of Jesus Christ, broaden our horizons and encourage our timid souls.

Forgive our blindness, Lord, and splash your light of faith across our lives...

Amen

READ LUKE 1:1-4, 4:14-21

REFLECT

Jesus returns to the hometown of his youth and attends synagogue on the Sabbath. He reads a prophetic declaration from the scroll of the prophet Isaiah: "The Spirit of the Lord is upon me..." (4:18).

As he sits down, those who listened to him read are quite impressed. They are amazed at his words, his delivery, the very presence he offers. They are so amazed that they have to remind themselves that Jesus is just the son of Mary and Joseph. Here is the Messiah, the Son of God, in their very midst. Yet, despite the fact that they are deeply moved, they are unable to free themselves to believe.

CONSIDER

- Why is this account important in the early ministry of Jesus?
- What human response leads Jesus' listeners to distrust and suspect him?

LET US PRAY

- For all those who read Scripture and offer us contemporary interpretations
- For open minds and open hearts to hear and heed God's Word
- For those who proclaim the Good News where Christianity has never been heard of
- For the passionate desire to nurture ourselves with the Word of God
- For our own personal intentions (shared with the group or held silently before the Lord)

A REFLECTIVE MOMENT OF SILENCE

ADDITIONAL ACTIVITIES/DISCUSSION

- How is Scripture often misused?
- When have we missed the presence of God in our midst?

Fourth Sunday in
ORDINARY TIME

They were all filled with fury.
Luke 4:28

WE GATHER IN PRAYER

Lord, open our eyes to see the goodness in everyone we meet. Let us recognize that each person has blessings and gifts and talents.

We want to be supportive of all people, day in and day out. May we never take for granted the ones we love most...

Amen

READ LUKE 4:21-30

REFLECT

Jesus reads the Scriptures and talks with the people in his hometown synagogue; his listeners are impressed. They speak well of him.

Then Jesus startles the folks by saying, in effect, that he is the Messiah. The people immediately change; they become angry and suspicious to the point of attempted murder. They just cannot believe that a "hometown boy" can be the one that Israel has been waiting for.

CONSIDER

■ What part of human nature is exhibited when we see the locals turn on Jesus?
■ What significance does this gospel have for our faith today?

LET US PRAY

■ For a respect for God's gift of human life in the womb
■ For a profound devotion to Jesus' presence in the tabernacle
■ For open minds and hearts, that we recognize God's goodness and wisdom, however and through whomever it may come
■ For all angry and disillusioned people
■ For our own personal intentions (shared with the group or held silently before the Lord)

A REFLECTIVE MOMENT OF SILENCE

ADDITIONAL ACTIVITIES/DISCUSSION

■ Would it be difficult for us to accept Jesus as the Savior of the world if he lived in our own neighborhood?
■ Why do groups of people turn into mobs when their collective expectations are not realized?

Fifth Sunday in
ORDINARY TIME

They left everything...
Luke 5:11

WE GATHER IN PRAYER

Lord, despite our weak faith, you love us unconditionally. Despite our failures to love, you never abandon us. Despite our fears and doubts, you plant the strength of your Spirit deep within our souls.

May we pull aside the curtain of our own sinfulness to see you waiting for us. May we have the courage to forgive ourselves and others while we look to a future of grace...

Amen

READ LUKE 5:1-11

REFLECT

The apostles know how to fish, when to fish, where to fish. Yet, their experience and skill fail them. Jesus, the carpenter, tells them how, when, and where to cast their nets—and the catch is astonishing. The catch confirms their trust in Jesus.

This incident follows Jesus' teaching the crowd from a boat. Jesus often uses miracles to demonstrate his power as God.

CONSIDER

- What do you think Jesus taught from the boat prior to telling the disciples to cast their nets?
- Compare the acceptance of Jesus as we see it in this gospel to the rejection of Jesus as it was portrayed in last week's gospel.

LET US PRAY

- For all who sail the seas and make their living in the fishing industry
- For environmentalists and forest wardens
- For those who are "fishers of people" for the sake of Jesus Christ
- For the courage to cast our nets as Jesus directs
- For our own personal intentions (shared with the group or held silently before the Lord)

A REFLECTIVE MOMENT OF SILENCE

ADDITIONAL ACTIVITIES/DISCUSSION

- "They left everything and followed him" (5:11). How do we follow Jesus today?
- Is our faith confirmed when we reflect on the many miracles of Jesus? Why or why not?

Sixth Sunday in
ORDINARY TIME

"Blessed are you...woe to you..."
Luke 6:20, 24

WE GATHER IN PRAYER

Lord, your Son's version of the beatitudes often differs from ours. He speaks of the poor and those who hunger as being truly blessed; we consider their plight unfortunate.

Bless our efforts to search for peace and happiness in the right places with the right intentions. Send the Holy Spirit to enlighten us and clarify our thinking...

Amen

READ LUKE 6:17, 20-26

REFLECT

How splendid to have been there during this discourse because we know "how the story ends." We know the ultimate truth of Jesus' identity and the salvation he brought into the world. The crowd listening to Jesus on that stretch of level ground, however, does not know the whole story. They hear "Blessed are you who are poor..." (6:20), and they are perplexed.

We know that the list of beatitudes is not a recipe for becoming poor. Jesus is not holding up poverty as a preferred condition. Rather, Jesus extends the first invitation to the world to develop a preferential option for the poor.

CONSIDER

■ What do the following phrases mean?
   "...the kingdom of God is yours" (6:20)
   "...you will be satisfied" (6:21)
   "...your reward will be great in heaven" (6:23)
   "...you have received your consolation" (6:24)
   "...you will be hungry" (6:25)
   "...you will grieve and weep" (6:25)

LET US PRAY

■ For all who are unhappy and seek satisfaction in empty places
■ For strength of character
■ For the courage and patience to suffer for Christ and the principles of Christianity
■ For a strong faith when our values are challenged
■ For our own personal intentions (shared with the group or held silently before the Lord)

A REFLECTIVE MOMENT OF SILENCE

ADDITIONAL ACTIVITIES/DISCUSSION

■ How do our priorities and life goals align with the beatitudes?
■ How do the beatitudes summarize the Good News?

Seventh Sunday in
ORDINARY TIME

"...a good measure, packed together..."
Luke 6:38

WE GATHER IN PRAYER

Lord, we are challenged to love everyone despite all odds. We are to love even our enemies. Yet, our homes, our places of work, our neighborhoods, are full of squabbles and tensions. Angry—yet insignificant—confrontations are routine.

Help us be truly loving and unselfish. Bless us with generosity... Amen

READ LUKE 6:27-38

REFLECT

Is Jesus really saying what we're hearing? Is this what it takes to be one of his disciples: love the unlovable? remain peaceful in the face of violence? respect the basics of justice when injustice strikes?

Yes! But Jesus is not suggesting that we be passive when confronted with hatred, violence, and injustice. Jesus is telling us that following him means to be concerned for the welfare of *all others*—even those who seem to perpetrate evil. Jesus insists on love, for only love can stop the plague of evil.

CONSIDER

- How are we, mere humans, to be merciful as God, almighty and all-powerful God, is merciful?
- Jesus says, "Give to everyone who asks of you..." (6:30). Do we take this command literally or figuratively?

LET US PRAY

- For all those who suffer injustice, that voices of justice will be heard on their behalf
- For all national leaders, that they may guide our planet toward nonviolent existence
- For those who work in the media, that their work be grounded in peace, not violence
- For inner peace
- For our own personal intentions (shared with the group or held silently before the Lord)

A REFLECTIVE MOMENT OF SILENCE

ADDITIONAL ACTIVITIES/DISCUSSION

- Who are the unlovable in our midst? in our community?
- How do justice and punishment work together—or do they?

Eighth Sunday in
ORDINARY TIME

"...the store of goodness...a store of evil..."
Luke 6:45

WE GATHER IN PRAYER

Lord, attitude and intention are important as we try to relate to you and others. We must not attempt to be someone or something that we're not. Humility is truth.

Help us to be genuinely humble. May we pray with simplicity and speak the truth in word and action...

Amen

READ LUKE 6:39-45

REFLECT

Jesus teaches in ways that jar the heart and leave the mind in a whirl. He teaches in parables. Below the surface of his stories, however, is wisdom for daily living.

Jesus points out that goodness gives birth to goodness and evil gives birth to evil (good trees bear good fruit; bad trees bear bad fruit). He cautions against hypocrisy (a hypocrite is a great pretender, especially about his or her own worth) and self-righteous (we see faults in others but fail to see ourselves as clearly).

CONSIDER

- How practical are these observations in everyday life?
- Why did Jesus teach in this manner?

LET US PRAY

- For the grace to see ourselves as God sees us
- For patience and humility when we are judged falsely
- For those of us who are prideful
- For the Truth that will set us free
- For our own personal intentions (shared with the group or held silently before the Lord)

A REFLECTIVE MOMENT OF SILENCE

ADDITIONAL ACTIVITIES/DISCUSSION

- Discuss the most common forms of hypocrisy in today's families and society.
- How can criticism be offered in loving ways?

Ninth Sunday in
ORDINARY TIME

They found the slave in good health.
Luke 7:10

WE GATHER IN PRAYER

Lord, we are encouraged to bring our needs to you. There is no doubt about your ability to respond. You are all-powerful and all-loving.

Yet, we approach with imperfect faith. May our spirits be stretched to embrace the faith of the centurion...

Amen

READ LUKE 7:1-10

REFLECT

The Roman centurion has his favor granted: his servant is cured. In asking Jesus, the centurion shows faith and humility. He says a prayer that we might adopt as our stance to all of prayer: "...say the word..." (7:7).

The centurion is not a Jew. Once again, we see faith and salvation offered to all those who believe.

CONSIDER

- What in the story indicates that the centurion is a man of faith even though he is not a Jew?
- Are some people faithful in their service to God even though they do not espouse Christianity? Why?

LET US PRAY

- For all those who are suffering with terminal illness
- For those who care, personally and professionally, for terminally ill people
- For all of us who are discouraged and desperate
- For the gift of faith
- For our own personal intentions (shared with the group or held silently before the Lord)

A REFLECTIVE MOMENT OF SILENCE

ADDITIONAL ACTIVITIES/DISCUSSION

- Read Matthew's account (8:5-13) and John's account (4:46-53) of this incident, and discuss the similarities and differences.
- Discuss miracles as they were understood two thousand years ago and as they are understood today.

Tenth Sunday in
ORDINARY TIME

He stepped forward...
Luke 7:14

WE GATHER IN PRAYER

Lord, you showed us how to be compassionate. Sensitive to the needs of others, you shared yourself.

They say that in times of great sorrow and joy, we should be particularly kind to others. Yet, daily kindness is our goal as well.

In our everyday lives, bless us with compassion for one another...

Amen

READ LUKE 7:11-17

REFLECT

Jesus is the only one who has ever stopped a funeral procession and called the deceased back to life. Imagine the reaction of the crowd at that moment. How joyful the widow must have been.

In this account, no one approaches Jesus and asks for a miracle. Jesus is simply moved by sadness and compassion for the widow's loss—and becomes involved. He takes the initiative, approaches the widow, tells her not to cry, and then shows her why she need not cry: her son is alive.

CONSIDER

- How does Jesus demonstrate the difference between offering new life and offering a helping hand?
- What effect does the account of this miracle have on our faith life?

LET US PRAY

- For a sympathetic spirit toward all who experience the death of a loved one
- For the courage to reach out to others without being asked
- For the humility to welcome the support and help of others when we are in need ourselves
- For the wisdom to recognize a miracle in our midst
- For our own personal intentions (shared with the group or held silently before the Lord)

A REFLECTIVE MOMENT OF SILENCE

ADDITIONAL ACTIVITIES/DISCUSSION

- What is our first reaction when confronted with the sufferings of others?
- Why do we often hesitate to "get involved"?

Eleventh Sunday in
ORDINARY TIME

"I have something to say to you."
Luke 7:40

WE GATHER IN PRAYER

Lord, we are taught to forgive. This is a good frame of mind. People came to Jesus with a change of heart; they were sorry. They reversed the direction of their lives.

Show us the way to contrition. Soften our hearts to offer forgiveness to others. Although we may feel deeply wounded, we want to imitate Christ in our willingness to be gracious and merciful...

Amen

READ LUKE 7:36-50

REFLECT

Jesus surprises many people because he associates with men and women known to be sinners. These associations actually aggravate some people. "He's a holy man. He ought to know better!"

Jesus is challenged at the home of the Pharisee. The woman touches him, bathes him, and dries him with her hair. She anoints Jesus' feet with ointment. Jesus explains that her sins are forgiven because she loves much. Her faith is her salvation.

CONSIDER

- "...the one to whom little is forgiven, loves little" (Luke 7:47). Discuss.
- How might Simon's life have been different after that evening with Jesus?

LET US PRAY

- For an appreciation of the many times Jesus forgives us
- For a good disposition of mind and heart toward those who offend us
- For global forgiveness; persons forgiving persons and people forgiving people
- For the passion to love much
- For our own personal intentions (shared with the group or held silently before the Lord)

A REFLECTIVE MOMENT OF SILENCE

ADDITIONAL ACTIVITIES/DISCUSSION

- Why does the charitable goodness of another sometimes disturb us?
- Are we afraid that forgiveness gives another the license to hurt us again?

Twelfth Sunday in
ORDINARY TIME

"...take up his cross daily..."
Luke 9:23

WE GATHER IN PRAYER

Lord, as followers of your Son, we identify with him. We are Christians. Jesus explains that following him means sacrifice. If we are not prepared to take up our crosses daily, we are not his followers.

Help us, Lord, to see that taking up the cross and following Jesus go hand in hand. May we realistically carry our crosses without some romantic idealism about suffering. May we love as you have taught us to love...

Amen

READ LUKE 9:18-24

REFLECT

"Just who do you think I am?" That is Jesus' question to his disciples. At first, he asks what the popular opinion is regarding his identity. People think he is great. They think he's a holy man. They hope he is the one destined to set them free: the Messiah. But their ideas are not clear.

In Jesus' exchange with his followers about his identity, he is quick to point out that suffering is part of his destiny. He knows that the Truth he brings to the world will endure only in the kingdom of God, not in the kingdom of this world.

CONSIDER

- What is there about Jesus that causes people to change their lives and follow him?
- Who do we say Jesus is?

LET US PRAY

- For the courage to act like followers of Christ
- For believers who are oppressed for their faith
- For a strong devotion to Jesus truly present in the tabernacle
- For the humility to admit when our faith is weak
- For our own personal intentions (shared with the group or held silently before the Lord)

A REFLECTIVE MOMENT OF SILENCE

ADDITIONAL ACTIVITIES/DISCUSSION

- What draws us to people who seem to know who they are, what they're doing, where they're going? Why?
- How have we allowed Jesus to make a major impact on our lives? in the world?

Thirteenth Sunday in
ORDINARY TIME

"...first let me say farewell..."
Luke 9:61

WE GATHER IN PRAYER

Lord, we are challenged to love unconditionally; there is to be no half-hearted efforts. This is the greatest of the commandments: to love you with our minds and hearts and souls. There is no substitute for total dedication.

Plant this orientation deep within our souls, Lord. Let nothing stand in the way of our seeking first the kingdom, your kingdom...

Amen

READ LUKE 9:51-62

REFLECT

The people of Samaria do not receive Jesus because he is on his way to Jerusalem. The feelings of hostility between Samaritans and Jews are deep and vicious.

Further down the road, Jesus meets people who are willing to follow him—to a point. Each has a reason, however, for not being able to stick with him.

Perhaps Jesus' responses seem harsh, but the point is made: the commitment to discipleship is an all-or-nothing journey. Even Jesus has a commitment to honor his Father's will. He has "set his face" toward Jerusalem and knows that there is no turning back.

CONSIDER

■ Discuss the "excuses" given in this gospel for not following Jesus.
■ Is Jesus being disrespectful of family obligations? Discuss.

LET US PRAY

■ For all people who have never seriously considered following Jesus
■ For those of us who have seriously considered following Jesus but struggle with nagging "excuses"
■ For contrition
■ For the wisdom to seek spiritual support when we need it
■ For our own personal intentions (shared with the group or held silently before the Lord)

A REFLECTIVE MOMENT OF SILENCE

ADDITIONAL ACTIVITIES/DISCUSSION

■ Discuss how Jesus never asks anything from his followers that he hasn't already done himself.
■ What are the "excuses" given today for not following Jesus?

Fourteenth Sunday in
ORDINARY TIME

"Carry no money..."
Luke 10:4

WE GATHER IN PRAYER

Lord, inspire us. Let us realize that there is more to life than eating, drinking, sleeping, and earning and spending money. There is a purpose to it all. That purpose is the one you have given us.

Just as Jesus sent his disciples out in pairs, we ask you to bless the spiritual companionship we share in this group. We journey together, toward you, in fellowship and support...

Amen

READ LUKE 10:1-9

REFLECT

Jesus sends his followers from town to town. They are to communicate love, forgiveness, and Truth. They will encounter difficulties. Some people will welcome them; others will shun them. There will be more work to do than they are able to accomplish. The harvest is more than they can handle—and the odds are stacked against them.

But God is on their side; they are about the kingdom of God. They are to continue despite the odds.

CONSIDER

- Does Jesus recklessly send his disciples into the surrounding villages: "...no money bag, no sack, no sandals; greet no one along the way" (10:4)? Why?
- What are the challenges to us today as we attempt to carry on Christ's mission?

LET US PRAY

- For all families, that they will know the peace and security of a faith community
- For all those who feel there is no purpose to life
- For missionaries who attempt to communicate God's goodness around the world
- For healthy vocations to all walks of life
- For our own personal intentions (shared with the group or held silently before the Lord)

A REFLECTIVE MOMENT OF SILENCE

ADDITIONAL ACTIVITIES/DISCUSSION

- Is there missionary territory right in our midst? Where?
- Discuss the gift of hospitality and the role it plays in the lives of those who take the Christian journey seriously.

Fifteenth Sunday in
ORDINARY TIME

"Take care of him."
Luke 10:35

WE GATHER IN PRAYER

Lord, effective prayer calls for action. We cannot merely say nice things to you and fail to respond to our neighbors' needs. There has to be involvement and investment.

Inspire us to be involved in the lives of others. There are those in our own community and in communities around the world who are hungry. There are those in our own community and in communities around the world who are caught in all forms of poverty.

Help us see with the eyes of love as we look for the needy in our midst...

Amen

READ LUKE 10:25-37

REFLECT

Jesus answers the lawyer's question with a parable: the Good Samaritan.

Our lives are "in good order" when we respect God's commandments. Yet, the challenge to love may make our lives feel anything but orderly, especially if those we love are despised by any portion of society. The story of the Good Samaritan articulates the involvement we are to have in loving all people.

CONSIDER
- How does Jesus demonstrate that loving may mean being "disloyal"?
- How can our lives "feel anything but orderly" when we choose to love?

LET US PRAY
- For the courage to seek justice for all, regardless of the circumstances
- For those trapped in poverty, that the vicious cycle is broken
- For a real desire to dedicate our lives to noble endeavors
- For all faith communities, that they will reach out to others without prejudice
- For our own personal intentions (shared with the group or held silently before the Lord)

A REFLECTIVE MOMENT OF SILENCE

ADDITIONAL ACTIVITIES/DISCUSSION
- How can good intentions and procrastination litter our Christian journeys?
- What are the positive and negative affects that tradition can have in our family, Church, and society?

Sixteenth Sunday in
ORDINARY TIME

"There is need of only one thing."
Luke 10:42

WE GATHER IN PRAYER

Lord, when we entertain visitors, show us how to welcome them in your name. Help us offer them genuine hospitality. Make our joy stem from their comfort.

May our homes be places to receive others as we would receive your Son. Bless our conversations. Let them be for your honor and glory.

May we treat our family members with the same graciousness and courtesy that we treat guests...

Amen

READ LUKE 10:38-42

REFLECT

Jesus spends time with friends who lived in Bethany, a small community about two miles from the city of Jerusalem. The sisters, Martha and Mary, welcome Jesus, although with somewhat different orientations. Martha concerns herself with Jesus' comfort; Mary concerns herself with Jesus' presence.

The truth of this gospel can be jarring.

CONSIDER

■ Why does Jesus say that Mary has made a good choice in what she is doing?
■ Does Mary exemplify the true disciple? If yes, how? If not, why not?

LET US PRAY

■ For all those who prepare meals, that they may know their efforts are appreciated
■ For the ability to listen with compassion and empathy
■ For the development of Christian prayer life, that we will all take the time for daily meditation and prayer
■ For those who are troubled, that they may find peace in speaking with Jesus
■ For our own personal intentions (shared with the group or held silently before the Lord)

A REFLECTIVE MOMENT OF SILENCE

ADDITIONAL ACTIVITIES/DISCUSSION

■ How can we, as individuals and as a group, be hospitable? (Consider certain jobs, civic involvements, and family activities.)
■ Should we try to balance the "Martha" activity in life with the "Mary" activity? If no, why? If yes, why and how?

Seventeenth Sunday in
ORDINARY TIME

"Lord, teach us to pray."
Luke 11:1

WE GATHER IN PRAYER

Lord, dissolve our occasional hesitancy to speak with you. Jesus teaches us to pray with confidence: "Our Father, who art in heaven...." He encourages us to ask so we might receive. He invites us into a trusting dialogue, an intimate relationship.

Bless us and bless our families with a confidence that makes our prayer truly powerful...

Amen

READ LUKE 11:1-13

REFLECT

Jesus' followers ask him the best way to address the heavenly Father. Jesus teaches them in the words that are so familiar to us today: the Lord's Prayer.

Jesus offers his followers an image of God that can be trusted. Ultimately, he stakes his life on that image and invites us to do the same.

CONSIDER

- What does each phrase of the Lord's Prayer mean in today's world?
- What is the relevance of this gospel for today's world?

LET US PRAY

- For those of us who struggle with prayer, that we may learn to communicate with the Lord
- For all those who help others to pray, that they may be blessed with patience and perseverance
- For all those on retreat, that they may be spiritually enriched and renewed as a result of their prayer time with Jesus
- For a spirit of prayer and reverence in our homes
- For our own personal intentions (shared with the group or held silently before the Lord)

A REFLECTIVE MOMENT OF SILENCE

ADDITIONAL ACTIVITIES/DISCUSSION

- What impact does prayer have on the pray-er?
- How would we respond to someone who says, "I've given up on prayer because I never get an answer"?

Eighteenth Sunday in
ORDINARY TIME

"Take care to guard against all greed."
Luke 12:15

WE GATHER IN PRAYER

Lord, we know that large bank accounts mean nothing in eternity. Yet, we often get caught up in the race to make money our life goal. Some of us aren't even aware that we're caught in this illusion.

Help us appreciate eternal treasures. Show us how to place you and your interests first in our lives...

Amen

READ LUKE 12:13-21

REFLECT

Jesus chooses this opportune moment to tell another story. He is asked a question about inheritance and, in response, cautions the crowd to beware of greed. He points out that one's wealth is not determined by one's possessions.

In the parable that Jesus tells, there is nothing that the rich man needs. Yet, he's not satisfied. He wants more—or at least he thinks he needs more. He is so taken up with worldly pursuits that he gives little time or attention to God.

CONSIDER

■ How is the rich man a member of the living dead?
■ Does this gospel imply that we should try to live in poverty? Discuss.

LET US PRAY

■ For those of us who feel burdened with financial obligations
■ For those who are rich, that they may use their resources and influence to help the poor
■ For our families, that our values will conform to Jesus' teaching about wealth
■ For a heart filled with appreciation for flowers, trees, fields, streams—God's treasures
■ For our own personal intentions (shared with the group or held silently before the Lord)

A REFLECTIVE MOMENT OF SILENCE

ADDITIONAL ACTIVITIES/DISCUSSION

■ Who are the poor in our community?
■ What is the general attitude toward money? How can we influence that societal attitude?

Nineteenth Sunday in
ORDINARY TIME

"...light your lamps..."
Luke 12:35

We Gather in Prayer

Lord, your Son tells us the way to live wisely. To embrace your grace means to be prepared for the moment when you call us home to yourself.

Bless our lives with a peaceful anticipation of eternity. Open our hearts to recognize the genuine good that constitutes the treasures of this life...

Amen

Read Luke 12:32-48

Reflect

Jesus wants us to think about the kingdom of God. He speaks about it often. He constantly urges us to work toward gaining lasting treasure.

Jesus' parable is presented in such a way as to make us think seriously about death. We do not know when it will come. But just as we can prepare for unexpected visitors to our home, we can prepare for God, who will one day visit us with an invitation to eternity.

Consider

■ How are we to act after reflecting on this parable? confident? timid? hesitant?

■ "Much will be required of the person entrusted with much, and still more will be demanded of the person entrusted with more" (12:48). What does this mean?

Let Us Pray

■ For sincerity as we try to live up to our Christian responsibilities

■ For the courage to examine our own hearts with regard to generosity

■ For a detachment from the things of earth and a desire for the things of heaven

■ For the development of the creative talents God has given each person

■ For our own personal intentions (shared with the group or held silently before the Lord)

A Reflective Moment of Silence

Additional Activities/Discussion

■ How can we prepare for death, both spiritually and practically?

■ What are we willing to risk for the treasures of the kingdom? Let's be specific.

Twentieth Sunday in
ORDINARY TIME

"...how I wish it were already blazing!"
Luke 12:49

WE GATHER IN PRAYER

Lord, when we find ourselves caught in controversies, wrap your wisdom around us. Give us the strength to be faithful to your Word. Teach us to hear the Truth within ourselves and in others.

Help us discern between steadfastness and stubbornness...

Amen

READ LUKE 12:49-53

REFLECT

When we take a stand for something, we automatically are taking a stand against something else. Unfortunately, the lines of opposition are not always clear-cut.

This gospel clearly states that Jesus will somehow bring division into our lives in ways that touch our hearts deeply. He uses the image of the family to convey just how savage that division might be.

CONSIDER

- Jesus says that he has not come to "establish peace on the earth" (12:51), yet we call him the Prince of Peace. Why?
- How would Jesus' words be received today?

LET US PRAY

- For all of us who actively pursue ways to grow in faith
- For those who suffer as a result of the contradictions within and among faith denominations
- For those who suffer alienation from their families, that they may experience acceptance and reconciliation
- For all who find religion boring and burdensome, that the Holy Spirit may enlighten them
- For our own personal intentions (shared with the group or held silently before the Lord)

A REFLECTIVE MOMENT OF SILENCE

ADDITIONAL ACTIVITIES/DISCUSSION

- Can we set aside a time to watch the movie *Romero* and discuss the cost of discipleship?
- What are the issues of faith today that tend to create division among people and within families?

Twenty-First Sunday in ORDINARY TIME

"Will only a few people be saved?"
Luke 13:23

WE GATHER IN PRAYER

Lord, bless us with the diligence and strength we need to walk the path toward your kingdom. Teach us how to cooperate with your grace as we struggle with tough choices in our complex lives.

May we never take your goodness for granted...

Amen

READ LUKE 13:22-30

REFLECT

While Jesus travels his way to Jerusalem, someone asks him about the number of those who will be saved. In response, Jesus does not offer a mathematical formula. Rather, he gives basic advice about the present: "Strive to enter through the narrow gate..." (13:24).

We often hear the expression, "The last shall be first and the first shall be last." Many expressions like this come from Scripture. Those who hear Jesus often think that the kingdom of heaven is exclusively for the Jews. But Jesus insists that the kingdom is for all: "And people will come from the east and the west and from the north and the south and will recline at table in the kingdom of God" (13:29).

CONSIDER

- How would we understand Jesus if he were talking to us in this Scripture reading?
- What is the meaning of "narrow gate"?

LET US PRAY

- For those of us who tend to be judgmental, that we will leave judgment in the hands of God
- For the strength and wisdom to pursue the narrow gate
- For the insight to realize that we glorify God in routine things when our hearts are set on eternity
- For the joy of a peaceful death
- For our own personal intentions (shared with the group or held silently before the Lord)

A REFLECTIVE MOMENT OF SILENCE

ADDITIONAL ACTIVITIES/DISCUSSION

- Do the Ten Commandments take on new meaning in light of this gospel? If yes, how? If not, why not?
- What does this gospel say about those who are not Christian?

Twenty-Second Sunday in
ORDINARY TIME

...choosing the places of honor...
Luke 14:7

WE GATHER IN PRAYER

Lord, teach us to be humble. Teach us to do things without ulterior motives. Teach us to recognize those opportunities in life when we can be genuinely humble: at home, in the workplace, in the broader community.

Bless our hearts with generosity. Just as we seek to please you by what we do and say, so inspire us to please one another by our quiet kindness...

Amen

READ LUKE 14:7-14

REFLECT

Jesus tells a story at the home of a Pharisee. The parable surely strikes the hearts of all listening. It hits home: "Don't look for the highest place, the position of honor. Take the lowest place. Be humble about it all."

As usual, Jesus talks about an upside-down-backward world where what we ordinarily anticipate is surprisingly turned around: places of honor are places of disgrace; entertainment becomes service; the nobodies are somebodies.

CONSIDER

- Is this parable a rebuke to those dining with Jesus and the Pharisee? Why?
- How do the usual social amenities of our society align with this gospel?

LET US PRAY

- For the grace to be like Jesus: meek and humble of heart
- For honesty with ourselves as we try to recognize our faults and correct them
- For the grace to understand that loving means giving without expecting anything in return
- For a genuine concern for the homeless and those burdened with the cycle of poverty and oppression
- For our own personal intentions (shared with the group or held silently before the Lord)

A REFLECTIVE MOMENT OF SILENCE

ADDITIONAL ACTIVITIES/DISCUSSION

- What is the difference between Christian humility and low self-esteem?
- Who do we consider truly humble? Why?

Twenty-Third Sunday in
ORDINARY TIME

"...unable to finish the work..."
Luke 14:29

WE GATHER IN PRAYER

Lord, teach us the true meaning of loyalty as your faithful followers. Give us the grace to recognize the sacrifices we must make to live a life of faith.

Turn our eyes to you as we feel the weight of our daily crosses...

Amen

READ LUKE 14:25-33

REFLECT

Jesus invites us to follow him. He declares clearly, however, that if we are not ready to make the sacrifices, we are not ready to follow.

It is particularly startling to realize that following Jesus might mean rejection within our families and neighborhoods. This makes us wonder if we have realistic expectations or romantic ideals about being disciples of Jesus.

Jesus insists that following him is a conscious choice; it isn't something we do by chance or for social acceptance. Twice in this gospel, Jesus explains the importance of careful calculation: "...sit down and calculate the cost..." (14:28) and "...sit down and decide..." (14:31).

CONSIDER

- What is the simple and practical realism in Jesus' advice?
- Is Jesus speaking literally or figuratively when he says, "...everyone of you who does not renounce all his possessions cannot be my disciple" (14:33)?

LET US PRAY

- For the courage to be disciples of Christ
- For those who need Jesus Christ for the conversion of their lives from drugs, alcohol, and other abuses
- For those of us who cling to social or professional prestige, that we will let go and turn to God
- For those of us who are lukewarm or indifferent in our faith, that our hearts will be enkindled with love for the Lord
- For our own personal intentions (shared with the group or held silently before the Lord)

A REFLECTIVE MOMENT OF SILENCE

ADDITIONAL ACTIVITIES/DISCUSSION

- Let's draft a job description for a disciple of Jesus.
- Why have we chosen Jesus as our personal Savior?

Twenty-Fourth Sunday in
ORDINARY TIME

"...I have found my lost sheep."
Luke 15:6

WE GATHER IN PRAYER

Dear God, fill our hearts with the same concern for sinners as Jesus displayed. Take us by the hand and lead us toward those most in need of patience, compassion, and understanding.

Open our eyes, Lord, to see that we are sinners ourselves...

Amen

READ LUKE 15:1-10

REFLECT

Jesus tells the story of the Lost Sheep to illustrate how we are welcomed back into God's unconditional love whenever we "stray."

As we reflect on this gospel further, however, we find ourselves both the topic of the gospel as well as the listeners: we are the sinners—and we are also to welcome the sinners with the same unconditional forgiveness and joy displayed by the shepherd who found the lost sheep and the woman who found the lost coin.

CONSIDER

- How does Jesus go out of his way to extend the love of God to sinners?
- Discuss the symbolism and imagery in this gospel (the shepherd, the sheep, the coin, the woman).

LET US PRAY

- For a gentle heart to forgive our enemies
- For those who are not on speaking terms with their families and friends
- For parents, that they will take seriously their obligation to guide their children toward Truth
- For a true appreciation of God's love for our brothers and sisters all over the world
- For our own personal intentions (shared with the group or held silently before the Lord)

A REFLECTIVE MOMENT OF SILENCE

ADDITIONAL ACTIVITIES/DISCUSSION

- How do we identify with the lost sheep in our daily lives?
- How do we welcome the lost sheep in our daily lives?

Twenty-Fifth Sunday in
ORDINARY TIME

"Prepare a full account..."
Luke 16:2

WE GATHER IN PRAYER

Lord, we thank you for the blessings that abound in our lives. You share your creation, and we are grateful. You trust us with your creation, and we are grateful.

Everything on the face of the earth is your creation, your gift. Teach us to respect that, to be caretakers of your treasures. May we be faithful and wise stewards...

Amen

READ LUKE 16:1-13

REFLECT

Jesus teaches with another parable. The dishonest steward thinks he is clever. Since he is about to be fired, he decides to feather his own nest. In a rash, dishonest sweep, he dismisses some of his master's debts to ingratiate himself to others—others who might lend him a helping hand when he hits hard times.

The Savior teaches that no one can serve two masters, especially if one is God and the other is materialistic.

CONSIDER

- Why does Jesus say, "...the master commended that dishonest steward for acting prudently" (16:8)?
- What does this gospel say about the poor?

LET US PRAY

- For all of us in our dishonest moments, that we will learn the kingdom value of honesty
- For those who are wealthy, that they will have the wisdom and courage to do good things with their resources
- For those who are poor, that they will not lose hope
- For all Christians, that we can understand Jesus' teaching about good stewardship
- For our own personal intentions (shared with the group or held silently before the Lord)

A REFLECTIVE MOMENT OF SILENCE

ADDITIONAL ACTIVITIES/DISCUSSION

- What is "mammon" in today's culture and society?
- How do we "serve mammon"?

Twenty-Sixth Sunday in
ORDINARY TIME

"If they will not listen..."
Luke 16:31

WE GATHER IN PRAYER

Lord, soften our hearts so that we don't go through life ignoring the poor and unfortunate. Show us how to be charitable and to appreciate the efforts of others who organize and reach out to those in need.

Bless us with the courage to participate in bringing justice into the world...

Amen

READ LUKE 16:19-31

REFLECT

This story is about a rich man who has it all and a poor man who suffers a great deal. The rich man fails to help the poor man. The rich man eventually goes to hell; the poor man goes to God and everlasting happiness.

Jesus uses this story to emphasize the fact that we need not *do something* to be guilty of great sin; more often, we are guilty when we *do nothing*.

CONSIDER

- What is it that the rich man *did not do* that determines his fate for eternity?
- What is the significance of the last line of the gospel: "If they will not listen to Moses and the prophets, neither will they be persuaded if someone should rise from the dead" (16:31)?

LET US PRAY

- For universal compassion, that we will all respond to the cry of the poor around the world
- For elected officials and government leaders, that they may legislate policies that foster justice
- For ourselves, that we will take our tax-paying responsibilities seriously
- For the homeless and all those who struggle with economic oppression
- For our own personal intentions (shared with the group or held silently before the Lord)

A REFLECTIVE MOMENT OF SILENCE

ADDITIONAL ACTIVITIES/DISCUSSION

- Does this gospel imply that the rich will not enter heaven?
- Does this gospel imply that the poor will definitely enter heaven?

ORDINARY TIME

"We are unprofitable servants..."
Luke 17:10

WE GATHER IN PRAYER

Lord, increase the faith of all people everywhere. This is the same request that the apostles made of Jesus.

We need your grace. We do not have the power and strength to withstand all challenges. Some trials and difficulties are too much for us to handle without faith in your abiding love and presence...

Amen

READ LUKE 17:5-10

REFLECT

Jesus assures his apostles when they ask him to strengthen their faith. He says that a little bit will go a long way. Mustard seeds are tiny. If the apostles have that small kernel of faith, they can move mountains.

Notice that Jesus does not use his faith to move mountains, however. He concentrates his power on the needs of the people. He heals, encourages, and loves.

CONSIDER

- What does the second part of this reading mean: "When you have done all you have been commanded, say, 'We are unprofitable servants; we have done what we were obliged to do' " (17:10)?
- Should we pray for more faith—or more love? Why?

LET US PRAY

- For our families, that we may all persevere in faith
- For those who doubt their faith, that they may be renewed
- For the courage and fortitude to be bold on behalf of justice
- For the strength to fulfill our obligations with joy
- For our own personal intentions (shared with the group or held silently before the Lord)

A REFLECTIVE MOMENT OF SILENCE

ADDITIONAL ACTIVITIES/DISCUSSION

- Do we have to affirm people for doing what's expected of them? Why or why not?
- How can we cooperate with the Spirit to increase our own faith?

Twenty-Eighth Sunday in
ORDINARY TIME

"...none but this foreigner..."
Luke 17:18

WE GATHER IN PRAYER

Lord, we know that giving thanks is important—not so much for your benefit but for our own. Giving thanks means recognition and acknowledgment.

Bless us with grateful hearts. May we give thanks in all things because of your faithful love for us...

Amen

READ LUKE 17:11-19

REFLECT

Jesus cures the incurable. Their leprosy is cleansed from their bodies. Only one, however, a Samaritan, returns to express gratitude. He falls to his knees and thanks Jesus.

Remember that the Samaritans are a despised group. Yet, it is the Samaritan who returns to express thanks and faith. We don't know why the other nine don't return with appreciation as well. We do know that Jesus wonders about this too: "Where are the other nine?" (17:17)

CONSIDER

- Give reasons why the other nine lepers did not return to thank Jesus for their miraculous cures: one reason for each leper.
- What is the significance of Jesus' question: "Has none but this foreigner returned to give thanks to God?" (17:18)

LET US PRAY

- For grateful hearts for the smallest blessings
- For all those who find relief in their suffering, that they will turn to God with praise and gratitude
- For humility, to express gratitude sincerely and accept gratitude gently
- For the courage to ask for what we need
- For our own personal intentions (shared with the group or held silently before the Lord)

A REFLECTIVE MOMENT OF SILENCE

ADDITIONAL ACTIVITIES/DISCUSSION

- Let's write a litany of blessings using "Lord, we thank you" after each blessing.
- Why do some people become angry when we try to help them?

Twenty-Ninth Sunday in
ORDINARY TIME

"Will he be slow to answer them?"
Luke 18:7

WE GATHER IN PRAYER

Lord, you want us to pray. It is your wish that we come to you for the graces and favors we need. This must be part of our spiritual formation.

We long to be in communication with you. Bless us with humility, openness, and respect as we come to you in prayer...

Amen

READ LUKE 18:1-8

REFLECT

The widow simply will not take no for an answer—nor will she allow the judge to ignore her.

Jesus uses this story to show us the importance of perseverance and hope. He does not compare the judge with God; he contrasts the two. If the judge finally gives in to the widow because he fears for his own well-being, imagine how quickly and lovingly God will respond to our hearts' needs.

CONSIDER

- The widow has *nerve*. Discuss the importance of "nerve" in living as a Christian.
- Why does Jesus ask, "...when the Son of Man comes, will he find faith on earth?" (18:8)

LET US PRAY

- For those who do not understand the value of prayer
- For those who misunderstand the value of prayer
- For all those who persevere for just causes
- For the "nerve" to be a committed Christian
- For our own personal intentions (shared with the group or held silently before the Lord)

A REFLECTIVE MOMENT OF SILENCE

ADDITIONAL ACTIVITIES/DISCUSSION

- Let's decide on just causes that we can pray for as a group.
- How can we persevere without becoming militant?

Thirtieth Sunday in
ORDINARY TIME

...convinced of their own righteousness...
Luke 18:9

WE GATHER IN PRAYER

Lord, pride is not a pleasing attitude for prayer. Soften our hearts with a humility that is pleasing to you. Whenever we worship, whenever we get on our knees to pray, settle our hearts in the right place: in quiet humility.

Help us to be sincere with ourselves, others, and especially with you...

Amen

READ LUKE 18:9-14

REFLECT

This is the parable about a Pharisee and a tax collector. The Pharisees held positions of esteem; the tax collectors were despised. In this story, Jesus makes the tax collector the "good guy." This man is humble, quiet, and genuinely contrite before the Lord. His posture before God is not haughty or prideful.

Once again, Jesus is emphasizing the importance of humility.

CONSIDER

■ How does the parable of the Pharisee and the Tax Collector affect the group that was listening to Jesus?
■ Does the tax collector know he goes home justified? Why or why not?

LET US PRAY

■ For the grace to be like Jesus: humble of heart
■ For a deep and holy reverence for the power of prayer
■ For women and men in offices of authority, that they may be faithful in Christian principles
■ For an appreciation for the privilege of serving others
■ For our own personal intentions (shared with the group or held silently before the Lord)

A REFLECTIVE MOMENT OF SILENCE

ADDITIONAL ACTIVITIES/DISCUSSION

■ How is our society both "Pharisee" and "tax collector"?
■ How can we confront a "Pharisee" without becoming one ourselves?

Thirty-First Sunday in
ORDINARY TIME

...and received him with joy.
Luke 19:6

WE GATHER IN PRAYER

Lord, let salvation come to our homes today. This is a blessing and a grace.

There is nothing more important than salvation; our lives literally hinge on it. We live now but look forward to eternity...

Amen

READ LUKE 19:1-10

REFLECT

Zacchaeus is curious about Jesus. He doesn't necessarily want to meet Jesus; he just wants to see him. Zacchaeus has heard that Jesus hangs around with the outcast folks in society—and Zacchaeus knows himself to be a notorious outcast. In fact, Scripture tells us he is the *chief* tax collector.

Zacchaeus gets his glimpse of Jesus—right in his own home. The result? Because Jesus reaches out to Zacchaeus with warmth and acceptance, Zacchaeus' entire life changes. He makes public amends for his transgressions, and salvation comes to his house "because this man too is a descendant of Abraham" (19:9).

CONSIDER

- Why does Zacchaeus want to see Jesus?
- What is the significance to the total gospel message of Jesus going to the home of Zacchaeus?

LET US PRAY

- For all of us who love God imperfectly, that God's grace will fill our hearts
- For generosity, that the miserly parts of ourselves will be overwhelmed with God's compassion
- For the willingness to forgive those who have cheated us in some way
- For the perseverance to learn what our tax dollars are used for and the courage to make changes where needed
- For our own personal intentions (shared with the group or held silently before the Lord)

A REFLECTIVE MOMENT OF SILENCE

ADDITIONAL ACTIVITIES/DISCUSSION

- Let's ask someone who has experienced a religious conversion to share their faith with us.
- How important is an attitude of acceptance in the life of a Christian?

Thirty-Second Sunday in
ORDINARY TIME

"...for to him all are alive."
Luke 20:38

WE GATHER IN PRAYER

Dear God, fill our souls with a sound faith in life after death. Keep the eyes of our souls on everlasting life. Empower us to follow your will.

Bless us with a proper perspective. May all our thoughts, words, and actions be performed for your honor and glory...

Amen

READ LUKE 20:27-38

REFLECT

The Sadducees do not believe in the resurrection; they believe in an eternity called Sheol, where all persons go regardless of their life choices and beliefs. With this orientation, the Sadducees are determined to undermine Jesus' credibility. They ask him about familial relationships after death.

Jesus jumps right into the exchange. Because he knows the reality of eternal life, he can tell the Sadducees that it simply doesn't matter: "...those who are deemed worthy to attain to the coming age and to the resurrection of the dead neither marry nor are given in marriage" (20:35).

CONSIDER

- What is the unique significance of verses 37 and 38 in this reading?
- Why does Jesus give the Sadducees his time and energy?

LET US PRAY

- For a loving and respectful detachment from earthly things and a sincere desire for eternal life with God
- For all those who suffer terminal illness, for their families, for their caregivers
- For the peaceful repose of the faithful departed
- For a good outlook on life, realizing that God longs to embrace us
- For our own personal intentions (shared with the group or held silently before the Lord)

A REFLECTIVE MOMENT OF SILENCE

ADDITIONAL ACTIVITIES/DISCUSSION

- Let's share our personal ideas about the afterlife.
- What are some healthy things we can say to those who express doubt about the resurrection of the body?

Thirty-Third Sunday in
ORDINARY TIME

"You will be hated..."
Luke 21:17

WE GATHER IN PRAYER

Lord, it pleases you when we have trust. There is a quality in children that is to be greatly desired. It is a childlike confidence. Jesus said that unless we become like little children, we will not enter the kingdom of heaven. It is good to think of this when we begin to be weighted with worries.

We rely on your loving care and compassion, Lord. We pray for the wisdom to turn to you quickly in times of challenge and temptation...

Amen

READ LUKE 21:5-19

REFLECT

The tone of this gospel is ominous. Jesus speaks about two things. He says that the magnificent Temple in Jerusalem will be destroyed—and it was. The Romans destroyed it in A.D. 70. The second destruction has to do with the end of the world.

Jesus also alerts his followers, once again, to the cost of discipleship. He knows his followers will be persecuted and tells them—us—not to lose heart.

CONSIDER
■ What does this gospel say about the challenges to a Christian?
■ Jesus is not trying to scare us. What is he trying to do?

LET US PRAY
■ For all of us who are fearful, that we hold on to hope and seek inner peace
■ For ourselves, that we may learn to trust in God's abiding presence
■ For those who are persecuted for their faith, that they may have strength and enlightenment
■ For all young people, that they grow stronger in their faith when challenges harass them
■ For our own personal intentions (shared with the group or held silently before the Lord)

A REFLECTIVE MOMENT OF SILENCE

ADDITIONAL ACTIVITIES/DISCUSSION
■ How would our faith be affected if we had the answers about God and suffering and the future?
■ What things are going on in the world today that look like the signs Jesus mentioned in this gospel?

CHRIST THE KING

"...this man has done nothing criminal."
Luke 23:41

WE GATHER IN PRAYER

Lord, we reflect on the scene of the crucifixion. We see in our imagination what happened on the hill outside of Jerusalem.

Jesus offers his life that we might have eternal life. This is a sacrifice motivated by unspeakable love.

As we meditate on the crucifixion, move our hearts with an abiding appreciation for the magnitude of your love...

Amen

READ LUKE 23:35-43

REFLECT

Jesus is crowned—not with jewels but with thorns. Jesus is cloaked—not with fine garments but with naked pain. Jesus is enthroned—not in stately royalty but on a cross in the company of two criminals. Christ our King.

One of the thieves crucified next to Jesus asks to be remembered when Jesus arrives in his kingdom. This man is not mocking Jesus; he is praying.

CONSIDER

- Why is this gospel read on Christ the King Sunday?
- Why does the feast of Christ the King officially "close" the Church year?

LET US PRAY

- For all criminals, that they will respond to the tender goodness of God that surrounds them
- For prisoners of war and those who suffer as a result of war, that they may all realize freedom and safety
- For the grace to enthrone Christ as king of our lives
- For the courage to claim our place in Christ's kingdom as we join in solidarity with the poor and those who suffer unjustly
- For our own personal intentions (shared with the group or held silently before the Lord)

A REFLECTIVE MOMENT OF SILENCE

ADDITIONAL ACTIVITIES/DISCUSSION

- How do we qualify as subjects in the kingdom of God?
- What similarities and differences are there between Jesus' birth and death?

FEAST DAYS

Husband of Mary
JOSEPH

...a righteous man...
Matthew 1:19

WE GATHER IN PRAYER

God, your grace and wisdom directed the intentions of Joseph. Faithful to you, he followed your lead as Mary's husband and the earthly father and protector of the Child Jesus.

We long to be as faith-filled as Joseph, to follow your lead in our chosen vocation. Open our hearts to hear the direction of the Spirit, that we may readily respond...

Amen

READ MATTHEW 1:18-21, 24

REFLECT

Joseph was a simple carpenter and faithful Jew. He knew the history of his people and longed for the coming of the Messiah—as did Mary. Loyal to the traditions of his faith and culture, Joseph was to take Mary as his wife. How disturbing it must have been to him to find that his beloved was with child. The human emotions of surprise, pain, and confusion were the same for Joseph as they would be for us today in similar circumstances.

With respect to Mary, Joseph planned to follow the custom of the time and quietly "break the engagement," as we would say today. Instead, he responds to the movement of God's divine love and, with Mary, answers "Yes" to the Spirit's invitation to participate in the history of salvation.

CONSIDER

- What were the primary virtues Joseph displayed in his decision to do "as the angel of the Lord had commanded him" (1:24)?
- How is the life of Joseph a model for all Christians?

LET US PRAY

- For all parents, as they raise their children in the faith
- For all those who struggle with the demands and disappointments of their chosen vocations
- For ourselves and our families, that we may model our faith after Joseph's
- For all those unable to hear or trust the promptings of the Spirit in their lives
- For our own personal intentions (shared with the group or held silently before the Lord)

A REFLECTIVE MOMENT OF SILENCE

ADDITIONAL ACTIVITIES/DISCUSSION

- How does the feast of Joseph, the Worker (celebrated on May 1) differ from the feast of Joseph, Husband of Mary?
- How might Joseph be a model for world leaders?

TRANSFIGURATION

"...his face changed..."
Luke 9:29

WE GATHER IN PRAYER

Dear God, the Transfiguration was an experience of recognition for the three apostles that were with Jesus. As they come out of their sleep, they see Jesus' radiance.

Bless us with the same awakening experience. Teach us to shake off the slumber that often grips our life of faith, to look for your radiance in the world around us, to be transformed ourselves...

Amen

READ LUKE 9:28-36

REFLECT

As Jesus moves toward the fullfillment of his mission, he takes several opportunities to question his followers regarding their understanding of his identity. In a few verses before the account of the Transfiguration, Jesus asks the discipes, "Who do the crowds say that I am?" and "Who do you say that I am?" (9:18, 20)

Jesus is compassionately aware of the human limits of his disciples. He knows the goodness of their hearts, but he also knows that they harbor misunderstandings about his mission and identity. When Peter, John, and James see "his glory" and hear the voice in the cloud say "This is my Son," their fear is turned to wonder and recognition.

CONSIDER

- Discuss all the possible emotions Peter, John, and James might have had during and after that experience.
- How does this Scripture relate to our faith journey today?

LET US PRAY

- For transfiguring faith, that we may know ourselves as sons and daughters of God
- For courage, that we may act on the faith we profess
- For wisdom, that we may recognize the transfiguring moments of our own lives
- For perseverance, that we may be faithful to our call to discipleship
- For our own personal intentions (shared with the group or held silently before the Lord)

A REFLECTIVE MOMENT OF SILENCE

ADDITIONAL ACTIVITIES/DISCUSSION

- Let's share our experiences of watching others come alive in their faith.
- How is our group being transfigured as a result of praying and sharing Scripture together?

Our Lady's
ASSUMPTION

"...my spirit rejoices in God..."
Luke 1:47

WE GATHER IN PRAYER

Lord, may we turn to you with praise in the tremendous moments of our lives as well as in the ordinary and routine. Lift our hearts with hope and anticipation even when life seems disappointing.

Bless us with the gift of spontaneous prayer, just as Mary burst with praise for your goodness. Someday, we hope to sing your praises for all eternity... *Amen*

READ LUKE 1:39-56

REFLECT

Mary is pregnant, yet she undertakes the long journey to visit her cousin, Elizabeth. When Mary and Elizabeth meet, joy quivers through the tiny infant in Elizabeth's womb; the first hosanna is sounded.

Mary's response is a spontaneous and innocent praise for God's boundless goodness and mercy. She doesn't clearly understand her role in salvation history, yet her faith energizes her and fills her with profound and prophetic praise. She knows the hunger for justice; she trusts in the mercy of God.

CONSIDER

■ Why has the Church chosen this passage for today's feast?

■ Why is the Assumption of Our Lady significant in the history of salvation?

LET US PRAY

■ For a deeper devotion to Mary, the Mother of Jesus, the Mother of the Church

■ For God's blessings on unborn infants, that their rights are protected by those who can speak for them

■ For families, that their joy in one another will proclaim the goodness of the Lord

■ For married couples, that grace will guide them in a life of passion and service

■ For our own personal intentions (shared with the group or held silently before the Lord)

A REFLECTIVE MOMENT OF SILENCE

ADDITIONAL ACTIVITIES/DISCUSSION

■ What are some accusations we've heard regarding our reverence for Mary? What might our responses be in the future?

■ How do we emphasize the significance of Mary in our personal faith journeys?

IMMACULATE CONCEPTION

...the virgin's name was Mary.
Luke 1:27

WE GATHER IN PRAYER

Lord, thank you for the model of faithful goodness you have given us in Mary. In her simple, quiet way, she responded "Yes" to your invitation to risk, to face the unknown, to love.

Fashion our hearts with the faith of Mary. Teach us to trust
your ways...

Amen

READ LUKE 1:26-38

REFLECT

Mary went about her quiet life with faith and hope. No doubt she had heard about the Promised One who would save her people from oppression—but little did she realize the role she would play.

Then the angel appears to her and invites her into an event that will change the world: "Behold, you will conceive in your womb and bear a son..." (1:31). To Mary, this is a confusing possibility because she isn't anyone's wife at the time. Yet, faced with public ridicule, Mary responds, "May it be done to me according to your word" (1:38).

CONSIDER

- Do we understand that the feast of the Immaculate Conception does not celebrate Jesus' conception in Mary's womb but Mary's conception in the womb of her mother?
- Why does the Church celebrate the conception of Mary?

LET US PRAY

- For a true appreciation of our baptismal vows
- For a devotion to Mary that reflects our trust in her role in salvation history
- For a willingness to respond "Yes" to all God's invitations
- For an appreciation of the Glorious, Joyful, and Sorrowful Mysteries
- For our own personal intentions (shared with the group or held silently before the Lord)

A REFLECTIVE MOMENT OF SILENCE

ADDITIONAL ACTIVITIES/DISCUSSION

- How has devotion to Mary changed over the years?
- Would we like to close this session with a decade of the rosary?

ALL SAINTS

"...your reward will be great..."
Matthew 5:12

WE GATHER IN PRAYER

Lord, how can we imagine the extent of peace and contentment you offer us? You created us from love, for love, for yourself.

Quiet our hearts to hear the wisdom of your words: from mountaintops to desolate street corners, may we hear your voice and understand your words...

Amen

READ MATTHEW 5:1-12

REFLECT

Jesus notices that he has a listening crowd. He takes the opportunity to summarize the Good News. To the surprise of his listeners, however, Jesus speaks of the privileged state of those considered the least privileged: the poor, those who mourn, those who are hungry and thirsty, those who are persecuted.

Jesus' listeners hear just the opposite of what they expected. In their state of poverty, hunger, and oppression, they are blessed. They are blessed as they mourn. They are blessed in their persecutions.

CONSIDER

■ How might Jesus word the beatitudes for today's listeners?
■ What is the significance of this event to the feast of All Souls?

LET US PRAY

■ For the wisdom to understand the rich truth of the beatitudes
■ For the courage to embrace the beatitudes as directives for life
■ For the humility to be truly poor in spirit
■ For merciful hearts, that we may offer the love of God to others
■ For our own personal intentions (shared with the group or held silently before the Lord)

A REFLECTIVE MOMENT OF SILENCE

ADDITIONAL ACTIVITIES/DISCUSSION

■ How have we adopted the beatitudes in our daily lives?
■ Let's discuss the "payoff" mentality that often plagues the Christian life: are we virtuous for our own gain or purely for the love of God?